Charles Tomlinson

The Sonnet

Its Origin, Structure and Place in Poetry

Charles Tomlinson

The Sonnet
Its Origin, Structure and Place in Poetry

ISBN/EAN: 9783337778170

Printed in Europe, USA, Canada, Australia, Japan

Cover: Foto ©Thomas Meinert / pixelio.de

More available books at **www.hansebooks.com**

THE SONNET.

THE SONNET

ITS ORIGIN, STRUCTURE, AND PLACE
IN POETRY

WITH

Original Translations from the Sonnets of Dante,
Petrarch, etc.

AND

REMARKS ON THE ART OF TRANSLATING

By CHARLES TOMLINSON, F.R.S.

LONDON
JOHN MURRAY, ALBEMARLE STREET
1874

TO THE

BARONESS BURDETT-COUTTS

IN GRATEFUL REMEMBRANCE OF

HER ACTIVE SYMPATHY

WITH THE AUTHOR DURING A GREAT TROUBLE

THIS VOLUME

IS RESPECTFULLY INSCRIBED.

PREFACE.

In this little book I endeavour to give some account of the Sonnet, and to compare the regular Italian form of that short poem with the English variety. I seek to prove that while the Italian Sonnet of the best writers, taking Petrarch as their exponent, is made up of several organic parts, each of which has its determinate function, and the result of the whole is a logical, consistent structure, the English form is generally more loose and inaccurate. My purpose is also to prove, from a critical analysis of some English translations of a number of Petrarch's best productions, that this great master of the Sonnet has not hitherto been properly represented in this country.

In the Second Part a number of Petrarch's Sonnets are arranged according to their metrical structure, serving to illustrate his three types and their variations, together with notes derived, to some extent, from a study of several of the best Italian commentators. I also venture to put forth my views as to the duties of a Translator; and although my attempts to render many of these celebrated productions into English are doubtless open to some of the censures that I so liberally bestow on others, yet I may claim for them this difference, namely, that they are so far distinguished from the performances of my predecessors as to be closer to the original, not only in their literal meaning but also in their metrical form.

My desire has been not to obtrude myself at the expense of my author; but, as far as possible, to reproduce his simple, eloquent, and beautiful language into equivalent expressions in our own tongue. I have also, in many cases, placed the original Italian by the side of my own work, so that the reader who has but a moderate knowledge of the language will, it is hoped, be able to derive instruction from this small performance in a not unpleasant form.

Some illustrative matter has been thrown into an Appendix, together with an attempt to support the opinion that the Laura of Petrarch was never married.

HIGHGATE, N., *May* 1874.

ANALYSIS OF THE CONTENTS.

PART THE FIRST.

                                                                                                    PAGE

1. Origin of this work—The regular Italian Sonnet—Its divisions into Quatrains and Tercets—Order of the Rhymes in the Quatrains or *Basi*—Enclosed and Alternate Rhyme   1

2. Order of the Rhymes in the Tercets or *Volte*—Interlaced and Alternate Rhyme   3

−3. The three hundred and seventeen Sonnets of Petrarch metrically arranged   3

        Type   I.—Number of Sonnets .   .   116
        Type   II.   ,,   ,,   .   .   107
        Type   III.   ,,   ,,   .   .   67
        Variations on the Three Types .   .   27
                                                            ——
                                                             317

    Order of the Rhymes in the Variations.

4. Illustration of Type I. from PETRARCH   5

    SONNET CCLXI.—*Levommi il mio pensier in parte, ov' era.*

5. DANTE's Sonnets metrically arranged   5

    SONNET from the *Vita Nuova—Negli occhi porta la mia Donna, Amore.*

6. Sonnets of MICHAEL ANGELO metrically arranged. . .   7

    SONNET XV. } *Non ha l'ottimo artista alcun concetto.*
      TYPE I.

7. Sonnets of TASSO metrically arranged   7

    SONNET LXV. } *Amore alma è del mondo.*
      TYPE I.

ANALYSIS OF THE CONTENTS.

	PAGE
8. Sonnets of ARIOSTO	8
9. Of VITTORIA COLONNA	8

10. Summary—Functions of the Quatrains and Tercets—Reference to the Greek Choral Ode—Derivation of the Sonnet traced to the Provençals—Various examples of complicated metre derived from them and adopted by Dante, Petrarch, etc.—Law which regulates the metre of the *Sestina*—The place of the Sonnet in poetry . . . 9

11. Origin of the Sonnet among the Italian Troubadours—Grounds for this Theory—Remarks thereon—The Jongleurs or itinerant singers—Petrarch's account of 17

12. The regular Italian Sonnet examined—Its logical structure—Differences between English and Italian poetry—Method of reading Italian poetry—Full lines 27

SONNET CCCXIII. } *I'vo piangendo i miei passati tempi.*
TYPE II.

13. Critical examination of this Sonnet—The laws of the Sonnet—Petrarch's Sonnet examined thereby—Difficulties of the Translator—Wordsworth's attempts to translate the Sonnets of Michael Angelo—Critical examination of one of Petrarch's inferior Sonnets 32

SONNET CCXXXI. } *La vita fugge.*
TYPE I.

Why this Sonnet is defective—Confusion of metaphor—Metaphor well sustained in

SONNET CLVI. } *Passa la nave mia.*
TYPE I.

14. Why the Alexandrine and the rhymed couplet at the end are objectionable 38

SONNET LXXXIII.—*L'aspettata virtu,*

in which a rhymed couplet is made to close the translation—Why this is wrong—This Sonnet resolved into a logical form.

15. Petrarch's Sonnets in the three types—Variations from these generally inferior—Some of the defects of Petrarch's Sonnets—Conceits and exaggerated language. . . . 41

ANALYSIS OF THE CONTENTS.

	PAGE
16. Dante free from these defects—Character of his Sonnets	43
17. Petrarch and Laura—Dante and Beatrice—Dante's love of philoscphy—His Sonnets	44

> Type II.—*Due Donne in cima delle mente mia.*
> And
> Type I.—*Nulla mi parrà mai più crudel cosa.*

18. The Laura of Petrarch and the Beatrice of Dante compared . 47

> Sonnet CLIX. } *Stiamo Amor, a veder la gloria nostra.*
> Type I.
>
> Dante. } *Di donne io vidi una gentile schiera.*
> Sonnet XIX.

19. Attention to method on the part of the great Sonnet-writers—Large amount of care bestowed on their Sonnets—Example from Dante 51

> Sonnet—*Vede perfettamente ogni salute.*
> The Author's gloss on this Sonnet—Example from Petrarch—Some account of his MSS. corrections—Extract from one of his letters, in which he describes his mode of working.

20. Character of the poetry thus elaborated—The poet's life at Vaucluse—True poetry of the Sonnets 56

21. How this poetry was influenced by chivalry—by the Troubadours, but mostly by the Platonic theory of love—Abstract of this theory 59

22. Influence of this theory on Dante's poetry—Extract from the *Vita Nuova*—Dante's account of Beatrice . . . 61

> Sonnet—*Tanto gentile e tanto onesta pare.*

23. The language of Petrarch's Sonnets defended—His power of expressing the feeling of bereavement—His record of Laura's death 65

> Sonnet CCCXVII } *Vago augelletto, che cantando vai.*
> Type II.

24. Early popularity of Petrarch's verses—Illustrated by an answering Sonnet 67

> Sonnet VII. } *La gola, e 'l sonno,* etc.
> Type III.
> Anecdote respecting this Sonnet.

xii　　　*ANALYSIS OF THE CONTENTS.*

　　　　　　　　　　　　　　　　　　　　　　　　PAGE
25. Petrarch's estimate of his Italian poetry 69
26. The Sonnet originally sung to music—Petrarch's lute—Great popularity of the Poet himself—Reasons which led the Poet to collect his Italian verses 70

　SONNET CCLII. ⎱ *S' io avessi pensato, etc.*
　　TYPE III.　 ⎰

27. Why the Sonnet is not popular in England, France, and Germany—The Song preferred 73
28. The best English Sonnets—Arrangement of Milton's Sonnets into Types 74
29. Wordsworth's Sonnets—Compared with the Italian . . 76
30. Revival of the Sonnet in England by Gray, Mason, Warton, Roscoe, Bowles. 79
31. Earlier Sonnet-writers—Spenser and Shakspere—The structure of their Sonnets—Raleigh—The Earl of Surrey—His Sonnet "Set me whereas the sun," etc., a translation from Petrarch—Sonnet CXIII., *Ponmi, ove 'l Sol, etc.*—The same in English—Surrey's version—Drummond—He borrows largely from Petrarch—Known as "the Scottish Petrarch"—One of his Sonnets compared with the 233d of Petrarch 80
32. Practice of our Early Poets of borrowing from the Italian Poets—Chaucer takes one of Petrarch's Sonnets—Spenser borrows from Tasso—Tasso from the Classical Poets—Supposed principle on which this practice rested—Changes that attended the decay of the practice—Anecdote of Piron—Modern examples 84
33. Petrarch borrows sparingly from the Latin Classics—Examples—Quotes from Holy Scripture several times—Examples 88

　SONNET LX. ⎱ *Io son si stanco, etc.*
　　TYPE III.　⎰

34. Petrarch's obligations to the Troubadour Poets—Example of a Sonnet suggested by one of them 90

　　　SONNET CIV.　　　　　　⎱ *Pace non trovo, etc.*
　First Variation of the Quatrains. ⎰

ANALYSIS OF THE CONTENTS. xiii

PAGE

Sonnet after the manner of the Troubadours—
SONNET CLXXXVIII. } *S'una fede amorosa, un cor non*
TYPE I. } *finto.*

35. The art of translating—*Metaphrase*, or literal rendering, and *Paraphrase*, or free rendering—Remarks by Dryden examined—Example from Petrarch 97

36. Impediments in the way of translating Petrarch's Sonnets into English verse — A line-for-line translation generally succeeds best — Illustration from the Tercets of Sonnet CXXVI. — Remarks as to the best mode of translating these lines 100

37. Necessity for literal rendering in single lines marked by their great poetical beauty—Illustrations by various hands— . 103
SONNET CCLI. } *Gli occhi di ch' io parlai si caldamente.*
TYPE II. }
Remarks on the mode of translating this Sonnet—The principle that ought to guide the Translator—Remarks by Voltaire, Diderot, and the Abbé de Sade—Dangers of what are called free translations illustrated by examples from this Sonnet.

38. Remarks on Petrarch's style — Its simplicity, directness, and clearness—Sparing use of adjectives— . . . 108
SONNET XXVIII. } *Solo, e pensoso, etc.*
TYPE I. }
as an illustration—Specimens of the mode in which this Sonnet has been translated.

39. Difficulties of producing translations that shall be adequate and popular — Faults in existing translations arising from five sources—(*a*) defective knowledge of Italian, whereby positive mistranslations are produced ; (*b*) substitution of the translator's ideas for the poet's, thereby leading to paraphrase ; (*c*) inelegant unpoetical English ; (*d*) general absence of attempts to reproduce the simple style of the original ; (*e*) want of attention to form and metrical arrangement—Numerous examples illustrating these defects . 112

40. A mistake to translate Petrarch in the language of gallantry —His reverential tone in writing of Laura illustrated by examples 129

SONNET CLXXXIV. } *Onde tolse Amor l'oro, etc.*
TYPE I.

Scanty use of the heathen gods and goddesses or of classical literature — Tone of the Sonnets during Laura's sickness—

SONNET CCXI. } *Qual paura ho, etc.*
TYPE I.

The Poet's tone after Laura's death—

SONNET CCLIV.
Second Variation of Quatrains. } *Soleano i miei pensier, etc.*
Tercets as in TYPE I.

SONNET CCCVIII. } *Non può far morte, etc.*
TYPE I.

41. An example of Petrarch's strong and indignant style . . 134

SONNET CV. } *Fiamma del ciel, etc.*
TYPE II.

42. Necessity for new translations of Petrarch's Sonnets—The principle upon which they ought to be made— . . 135

43. The translator should follow Petrarch in his mode of working 135

44. Necessity for studying in Petrarch's life, letters, etc., the circumstances under which each Sonnet was produced . 137

45. Qualifications of a poet and of a translator 138

46. Best method of translating—Advantages to the translator . 138

47. Necessity for consulting the Italian commentators—Illustrated by an extract from the 241st Sonnet — Another example from the 51st Sonnet 139

48. Conclusion 143

PART THE SECOND.

ILLUSTRATIONS FROM PETRARCH OF THE THREE TYPES AND THEIR VARIATIONS.

Note on the Numbering of Petrarch's Sonnets.

TYPE I.

SONNET
1. *Voi, ch' ascoltate in rime sparse il suono.* Annotation . 147
48. *Padre del Ciel, dopo i perduti giorni.* Do. . 148

ANALYSIS OF THE CONTENTS. xv

SONNET		PAGE
71.	On the death of Cino. *Piangete, donne.* Annotation, with a Sonnet by Cino	150
111.	*Quand 'io v' odo parlar si dolcemente*	151
112.	*Nè così bello il Sol giammai levarsi.*	152
143.	*Per mezz' i boschi inospiti.* Annotation . . .	152
210.	*Chi vuol veder quantunque puo Natura* . . .	153
247.	*I' ho pien di sospir quest' aer tutto.* Annotation .	154
260.	*Valle, che de 'lamenti miei se' piena.* Do. . .	155
261.	*Levommi il mio pensier in parte.* Do. . .	156
262.	*Amor, che meco al buon tempo ti stavi.* Do. .	158
268.	*L' alto, e novo miracol.* Do. . .	159
283.	*L' aura, e l' odore, e l' refrigerio.* Do. . .	162
289.	*Vide fra mille Donne una gia tale.* Do. . .	163
291.	*Questo nostro caduco, e fragile bene.* Do. . .	164
303.	*Donna, che lieta col principio nostro* . . .	165
306.	*L' aura mia sacra*	165

Type II.

173.	*Rapido fiume, che d' alpestra vena.* Annotation on the use of technical words in poetry	166
205.	*Fresco, ombroso, fiorito, e verde colle* . . .	169
246.	On the death of Sennuccio. *Sennuccio mio.* Annotation, with a Sonnet from Fra Guittone . . .	169
264.	*Anima bella, da quel nodo sciolta.* Note . .	171
269.	*Zefiro torna, e 'l bel tempo rimena* . . .	172
279.	*Sento l' aura mia antica.* Note . . .	173
295.	*Conobbi, quanto il Ciel gli occhi m'aperse.* Annotation .	173
299.	*Ripensando a quel*	175
302.	*Gli Angeli eletti, e l' anime beate* . . .	175

Type III.

25.	*Quanto più m' avvicino.* Annotation . . .	176
69.	*Erano i capei d' oro.* Do. . . .	177
80.	*Lasso! ben so.* Do. . . .	179
248.	*L' alma mia fiamma.* Do. . . .	180
307.	*Ogni giorno mi par.* Do. . . .	181

First Variation of the Quatrains.

59.	*S' al principio risponde il fine.* Note . . .	182
240.	*Quante fiate al mio dolce ricetto.* Do. . . .	183

ANALYSIS OF THE CONTENTS.

SONNET		PAGE
	SECOND VARIATION OF THE QUATRAINS.	
238.	*Se lamentar augelli.* Note	184
	THIRD VARIATION OF THE QUATRAINS.	
175.	*Non dall' Ispano Ibero all' Indo Idaspe.* Annotation	185
	FIRST VARIATION OF THE TERCETS.	
76.	*Ahi! bella Liberta!*	187
109.	*Amor, che nel pensier mio.* Annotation, together with an Abstract of Michael Angelo's Lecture on this Sonnet	187
241.	*Alma felice, che sovente torni.* Annotation . .	193
270.	*Quel rosigniuol, che si soave piagne.* Do. . .	194
	SECOND VARIATION OF THE TERCETS.	
72.	*Più volte Amor m' avea già detto: Scrivi.* Annotation	196
	THIRD VARIATION OF THE TERCETS.	
73.	*Quando giugne per gli occhi.* Annotation . .	198
	FOURTH VARIATION OF THE TERCETS.	
74.	*Cosi potess' io ben chiuder in versi.* Note . .	199

APPENDIX.

I.	SESTINA FROM PETRARCH. *Chi è fermato di menar sua vita*	201
II.	MADRIGAL FROM PETRARCH. *Perch' al viso d' Amor portava insegna*	203
III.	BALLATA FROM PETRARCH. *Perchè quel, che mi trasse ad amar prima*	203
IV.	MADRIGAL FROM PETRARCH. *Or vedi, Amor, che giovenetta Donna*	204
V.	MADRIGAL FROM PETRARCH. *Nova angeletta sovra l'ale accorta*	205
VI.	ON THE LITERARY HABITS OF PETRARCH'S TIME .	205
VII.	ON THE IDENTIFICATION OF LAURA . . .	209
VIII.	ALLEGORY ON LAURA. SONNET CLVII. TYPE I. *Una candida cerva sopra l' erba.* Explanation of this Sonnet	223
IX.	GERMAN TRANSLATIONS OF PETRARCH'S SONNETS .	225

TO THE READER.

The dark-eyed stranger from yon sunny clime,
   An exile 'neath our colder, cloudier skies,
   For native brightness, native gladness sighs,
   And the soft speech that yields the softer rhyme;
Sighs for the Love he knew in happier time,
   In the responsive sunshine of her eyes;
   Sighs 'midst the coldness of the worldly-wise,
   Who dull their sense of beauty in their prime.
So these sweet sonnets, in my rougher speech,
   As exiles, lose their native loveliness,
   The tones unheard of Dante's, Petrarch's lyre;
But should they lead thee upwards, 'till thou reach
   Their burning source, to greater from much less,
   I need not blush for my reflected fire.

PART THE FIRST.

AN ESSAY ON THE SONNET:

ITS ORIGIN, STRUCTURE, AND PLACE
IN POETRY.

PART THE FIRST.

1. IN the winter of the year before last, finding myself in the presence of a great and abiding grief, I felt the need of some kind of employment that could be taken up and laid down as best suited the occasion, without injury to it or to my power of mastering it; and at the same time sufficiently difficult to absorb my best attention. Among my avocations in previous years, I had read a good deal of Italian poetry, and had several times attempted to enter into the spirit of Petrarch's sonnets, but without much success. The occasion seemed to be now more favourable to a better appreciation of these famous productions, especially in the second part. The gentle being who had engaged some of the best thoughts of Petrarch's life was dead, and the varied notes of sorrow poured out by him became grateful to me. I attempted to translate some of these sonnets into English verse as literally as possible, and with the same metrical arrangement. From these I was led to examine similar compositions by the best Italian writers, such as Dante, Tasso, Ariosto, Michael Angelo, and Vittoria Colonna.

I need hardly remark that I found the poetical value of these sonnets worthy of their fame; but what claimed my attention also was their greater precision in structure, as compared with the sonnets of our English masters—a precision which gives to the regular Italian sonnet a peculiar place in poetry, unlike that of any other established form of modern lyric, for no other form is bound by such rigid rules. The sonnet, according to the regular Italian type, resolves itself into an octave of eight lines and a sestet of six; these being further subdivided into two quatrains and two tercets, each of the two separate parts having its own system of rhymes. Thus the most common form for the quatrains is for the first line to rhyme with the fourth, the fifth, and the eighth, and the second line with the third, the sixth, and the seventh; or as the arrangement may be more concisely expressed in the formula—

$$1 \quad 2 \quad 2 \quad 1$$
$$1 \quad 2 \quad 2 \quad 1$$

The quatrains are sometimes named the *Basi*, or "bases" of the sonnet, and the above arrangement is known as *rima chiusa*, or "shut-up" or "enclosed rhyme."

The second mode of arranging the quatrains is in *alternate* rhyme, as in the following formula:—

$$1 \quad 2 \quad 1 \quad 2$$
$$1 \quad 2 \quad 1 \quad 2$$

This structure is more sparingly used than the first, and is occasionally varied thus—

        1   2   1   2
        2   1   2   1

2. The tercets, or *volte* or "turnings," as they are sometimes named, have much greater powers of variation in their rhymes than the quatrains. They may be either in *rima incatenata*, or "interlaced," or "interlocked" rhymes; or *rima alternata* or "alternate" rhymes. Of the former, the arrangement

        3   4   5
        3   4   5

is the most common; varied by

        3   4   5
        4   3   5

or by

        3   4   5
        3   5   4

and several others, which must, however, be regarded as exceptional.

3. I took the trouble to make a metrical arrangement of the three hundred and seventeen sonnets of Petrarch, and to place them in a tabular form according to the order of the rhymes. The result of this analysis is that one hundred and sixteen sonnets, or upwards of one-third of the total number, belong to

what I venture to name TYPE I., or the *normal Italian type*, as expressed by the formula—

$$\text{Type I.} \begin{cases} 1 & 2 & 2 & 1 & 1 & 2 & 2 & 1 \\ & 3 & 4 & 5 & 3 & 4 & 5 \end{cases}$$

Upwards of another third, or one hundred and seven sonnets, have the tercets alternately rhymed, and this arrangement, which may be named TYPE II., has the formula—

$$\text{Type II.} \begin{cases} 1 & 2 & 2 & 1 & 1 & 2 & 2 & 1 \\ & 3 & 4 & 3 & 4 & 3 & 4 \end{cases}$$

In sixty-seven sonnets the metrical arrangement is according to the formula—

$$\text{Type III.} \begin{cases} 1 & 2 & 2 & 1 & 1 & 2 & 2 & 1 \\ & 3 & 4 & 5 & 4 & 3 & 5 \end{cases}$$

Now it will be seen that in the three types, which include two hundred and ninety out of three hundred and seventeen sonnets, the variations are but slight. The structure of the quatrains is the same in all three types, and in the tercets three lines rhyme with three lines. Of the remaining twenty-seven sonnets, which do not fall under any one of the three types already given, the quatrains in eleven sonnets are arranged as in the three types; in another eleven they are in alternate rhyme, and in the remaining four they are arranged thus—

$$1 \; 2 \; 1 \; 2 \; 2 \; 1 \; 2 \; 1$$

As to the arrangement of the tercets, many of them follow one or other of the first three types, and a few fall under one or other of the following formulæ :—

$$3\ 4\ 3,\ 3\ 4\ 3$$
$$3\ 4\ 4,\ 4\ 3\ 3$$
$$3\ 4\ 5,\ 5\ 4\ 3$$
$$3\ 4\ 5,\ 4\ 5\ 3$$

4. Of the first or normal type, the following translation from Petrarch may serve as an illustration :—

SONNET CCLXI. } *Levommi il mio pensier in parte,*
TYPE I.   }   *ov' era.*

On wings of thought I soared to regions where
  She whom I seek, but here on earth in vain,
  Dwells among those who the third heaven gain,
  And saw her lovelier and less haughty there.
She took my hand and said—" In this bright sphere,
  Unless my wish deceive, we meet again :
  Lo! I am she who gave thee strife and pain,
  And closed my day before the eve was near.
My bliss no human thought can understand :
  I wait for thee alone—my fleshly veil,
  So loved by thee, is by the grave retained."
She ceased, ah why! and why let loose my hand!
  Such chaste and tender words could so prevail,
  A little more, I had in heaven remained.

5. Dante, who is perhaps the greatest master of the modern Italian sonnet, has about forty specimens which are regarded as authentic. The quatrains in

thirty-three examples are regular, as in Types I., II., and III., and alternate in the remaining seven. Of the tercets connected with the former, eleven sonnets are thus arranged—3 4 5 4 3 5. In eight examples they are alternate. In another eight—3 4 5 5 4 3. In six—3 4 4 4 3 3; and in four—3 4 3 3 4 3. In the second case, where the quatrains are in alternate rhymes, the tercets are in five cases arranged as in Type I., as if to avoid monotony. In one case they follow this order—3 4 5 5 4 3; and in one only are they alternate.

As an illustration of Dante's mastery over the sonnet, I give the following from the *Vita Nuova*, with the remark that Dante's sonnet poetry is so beautifully simple and direct that the verses often seem to translate themselves, as in several of the lines of this poem, especially the first:—

1 2 2 1, 1 2 2 1 } *Negli occhi porta la mia Donna,*
3 4 5, 5 4 3 }   *Amore.*

My lady carries love within her eyes,
   And thus makes gentle whom she gazes on;
   Where'er she goes, all men towards her turn;
   Whom she salutes, trembles his heart somewise,
And conscious of his own defects, he sighs,
   With downcast look, and countenance all wan:
   Before her, anger, pride, are quickly gone:
   O aid me, ladies! to set forth her praise.
Who hears her speak, feels something come to bless,
   For, in his heart, sweet, lowly thoughts are bred;

He's blest who first beholds her for awhile :
But how she looks if she but gently smile,
  Cannot be kept in mind, still less be said,
  New miracle is she of gentleness.

6. Of the eighty complete examples of the sonnet left by Michael Angelo, seventy-one fall under the metrical arrangement of Type I., eight under Type II., and one only in which the rhymes both in the quatrains and the tercets are alternate. The following is from this master :—

SONNET XV. } *Non ha l'ottimo artista alcun concetto.*
TYPE I.

Hid in the marble, there already lies
  Whate'er the greatest sculptor can design :
  He only sets it free from its rude shrine,
  Whose hand skill guides what intellect supplies.
The ill I flee, the good I so much prize,
  In thee, O lady! fair, yet proud, divine,
  Thus hidden lie ; and that in death I pine,
  Reverse effects, from those intended, rise.
Love then is not to blame for ills I feel,
  Nor yet thy beauty, hardness, high disdain ;
  I blame not chance nor my hard destiny :
If death and life thou in thy heart conceal,
  I, all unskilled, though loving, seek in vain
  To draw forth life, I death alone set free.

7. My edition of Tasso contains two hundred and twenty-three sonnets. Of these sixty-four belong to Type I., thirty-four to Type II., and forty-four to Type III. Of the remaining eighty-one, the quatrains are

regular in seventy-one examples. As to the tercets, they are thus arranged in twenty-six examples:—3 4 5 5 4 3; and in twelve thus—3 4 5 4 5 3; and in fifteen—3 4 5 3 5 4; and in eighteen—3 4 5 5 3 4. Tasso deals but little in alternate rhymes. The following is an illustration of his style:—

TYPE I.—*Amore alma è del mondo, Amore è mente.*

Love is the soul of the world, and Love is mind;
   He guides the sun obliquely on his way;
   The planets dance to his lyre's celestial play,
   As swift or slow the measure is combined.
He rules earth, fire, the waters, and the wind,
   In the vast body mingled; 'neath his sway
   All things are nourished; men are sad or gay,
   And hopes, delights, and cares, and dolours find.
Though Love creates all things, o'er all is king,
   In all resplendent, brightness making bright,
   And of our lives makes up the greater part;
Why need we seek him on celestial wing,
   Since he has fixed his palace in the light
   Of thy sweet eyes, his temple in this heart?

8. Ariosto has not composed a large number of sonnets; but most of them are constructed according to Type II., and a few of them are *codati*, or tailed.

9. Taking the first hundred sonnets of Vittoria Colonna, the same respect for established types is to be observed. Forty-six follow Type I., eighteen Type II., and forty-six Type III. In the remainder

the quatrains are all regular; but the tercets are more varied.

10. The conclusion to be drawn from these statements is, that the Italian sonnet is a poem of regular construction. It is not what some of our best English poets make it, namely, a short continuous poem, running through, from the first line to the last, in almost any order, and winding up with a couplet; but built up of parts or quatrains, the *Basi* or bases of the structure; and of tercets or *Volte*, turnings or roads to which the *basi* point. Moreover, each quatrain has its peculiar office or function, as well as each tercet, and hence they should be kept distinct, and not be run into each other,—as distinct as the separate parts of the Greek choral ode, which has been supposed by some to be the parent of the regular Italian sonnet; the first quatrain being equivalent to the strophe, the second to the antistrophe; the first tercet to the epode, and the second tercet to the antepode. But the more usual theory is that the sonnet originated with the Provençal poets in common with the *canzone*, and many other forms, in which the structure is bound by so many conditions of versification that it seems marvellous how the thought could ever be moulded by the writer or find its way to the mind of the reader or auditor. As the words *sonetto* and *canzone* imply (from *piccol suono*, a small sound or composition, and *dal canto*), they were sung with a musical accompaniment, in

common with all lyric poetry, and had reference to the composer's own thoughts and feelings. As the Horatian lyrics merged into the rhyming verses of the monks, and scansion gave way to accent, these probably gave rise to the poems of the troubadours (*trovatori, i.e.* inventors) of the early part of the eleventh century. The rules of versification by which the perfect models of Horace were guided were not understood; but, as it was evident that some rules were necessary, these were framed with reference to the arrangement of verses and of rhymes, often of a complicated and fantastic character. Such a Latin couplet as the following:

> Cena brevis, vel cena levis, fit raro molesta;
> Magna nocet, medicina docet; res est manifesta,

would be sure to please a people in the rudiments of a reviving literature by its ringing rhymes, and find numerous imitators in the modern tongue. In this way the ear became fascinated with frequent rhymes, and, as they grew more and more familiar, it was held to be a feat to make their arrangement difficult, and to introduce them into unexpected places in the verse. Even such great masters of versification as Dante and Petrarch were to some extent bound by the prevailing fashions, and produced poems which are perfect marvels of complication. For example, Petrarch's sixth *Canzone, Verdi panni*, etc., consists of eight stanzas of seven lines each, and the rhymes are so distributed that the corresponding lines of the several stanzas rhyme together—thus the 1st line of the first stanza rhymes with the 1st line of the second . . . . 8th, and so on of all the other lines. But this is not the only difficulty; the beginnings of the 4th and 6th lines of the first stanza give rhymes to the beginnings of the 4th and 6th lines of all the succeeding stanzas. The poem winds up with an *envoi* or *commiato*[1] of two lines, rhyming with the 6th and 7th lines of the preceding stanzas. Petrarch's Canzone XXII., *Mai non vo' piu cantar*, is a wonderful example of the power of rhyming given by the Italian language. There are six stanzas of fifteen lines each, and the terminal rhymes are thus arranged in each stanza—1 2 3 1 2 3 4 5 4 4 5 6 7 7 6. But, in addition to this, the last word of each line rhymes with a word in the middle of the next line:

> *Mai non vo' piu cantar, com' io soleva*
> *Ch' altri non m' intendeva; ond' ebbi scorno*
> *E puossi in bel soggiorno esser molesto.*

But, for the sake of variety, the rule is not observed in the 10th and 14th, which are short lines, nor in the 4th, 13th, and 15th lines. In contrast to this wealth of rhyme, is Petrarch's 34th *Canzone, S'il dissi mai*, of six stanzas of nine lines each, and a

---

[1] The *commiato*, or "leave-taking," often consists of half a stanza, in which the poet addresses his composition, says what he expects of it, and wishes it good speed.

refrain or *commiato* of four lines, and only three rhymes in the whole poem; while the words *S'il dissi* are repeated at the beginning of the 1st, 3d, and 5th lines of each of the first four stanzas, and dismissed at the 5th with *Ma s'io nol dissi*. The rhymes of the first stanza are thus arranged—

      1 2 2 1 1 3 3 3 1

But most remarkable for complication is that variety of the *canzone* known as the *sestina*, which, as its name implies, consists of six stanzas, each stanza of six lines, and the terminal words of the first stanza also form the terminations of the lines of all the other stanzas, but in a different order; only with this condition, that the last word of each stanza must be the terminal of the first line of the next. Not being able to find in Crescimbeni, or any similar authority, on what principle the terminal words of the various stanzas are arranged, I took one of Dante's sestinas, *Amor mi mena*, etc., and arranged the terminal words of each stanza in horizontal lines, and also in vertical lines. This produced a certain harmonious arrangement, which satisfied me that some principle of selection overruled this *sestina;* and having obtained the same result in other *sestine*, I was able, with the assistance of my mathematical friend, Mr. Walenn, to state the following law of the composition, namely:—That each stanza is formed from the previous one; and if 1 2 3 4 5 6 be the order of the terminal words of the previous stanza, the order of the words in the stanza in question is 6 1 5 2 4 3. Thus, in all three of Dante's sestinas, the terminal words in the first stanza are—

1, *ombra;* 2, *colli;* 3, *erba;* 4, *verde;* 5, *pietra;* 6, *donna.*

Then, according to the rule, these words are thus arranged in the second stanza—

6, *donna;* 1, *ombra;* 5, *pietra;* 2, *colli;* 4, *verde;* 3, *erba.*

The words thus arranged in the second stanza now control the arrangement in the third stanza; but before applying the rule, the words as they stand in the order 6 1 5 2 4 3, without disturbing that order, must be re-numbered 1 2 3 4 5 6; and from this re-numbering, the rule for the arrangement of the third stanza is to be applied thus—

3, *erba;* 6, *donna;* 4, *verde;* 1, *ombra;* 2, *colli;* 5, *pietra,*

and so on for the remaining stanzas.

The law or rule in question may also be thus stated:—The terminations of the alternate even lines of each stanza follow the sequence of the previous stanza in direct order; and the terminations of the alternate odd lines of each stanza follow the sequence of the previous stanza in inverse order. Thus the second, fourth, and sixth lines of every stanza have respectively the same terminations as the first, second, and third lines of the previous stanza; and the first, second, and third lines of any stanza have respectively the same terminations as the sixth, fifth, and fourth of the previous stanza.

In order that the reader may test the application of these rules, I give the six terminal words of Petrarch's 36th *Canzone, Anzi tre dì,* etc., as they occur in all six stanzas, and in the final *commiato,* in which, as is usual, three of the words are at the end, and the other three in the middle of the lines.

Stanza 1.	2	3	4	5	6	Commiato.
parte	*bosco*	*pregio*	*sciolta*	*corso*	*nove*	*nove*
nove	*parte*	*bosco*	*pregio*	*sciolta*	*corso*	*corso*
pregio	*sciolta*	*corso*	*nove*	*parte*	*bosco*	*bosco*
corso	*nove*	*parte*	*bosco*	*pregio*	*sciolta*	
sciolta	*corso*	*nove*	*parte*	*bosco*	*pregio*	
bosco	*pregio*	*sciolta*	*corso*	*nove*	*parte*	

There are also double *sestine* of twelve stanzas, such as Petrarch's 46th *Canzone, Mia benigna fortuna,* etc. These follow the same law, and the second half is a repetition of the first so far as the arrangement of the terminal words is concerned. There are also triple *sestine* of eighteen stanzas each; and *sestine* with twelve lines to each stanza, as in Dante's 10th *Canzone, Amor tu vedi ben,* etc. In these last the terminals of each line are formed from those of the previous stanza, according to a fixed law; the terminal of the last line of each stanza being also the terminal of the first line of the next. In the example just cited there are but five distinct terminals in the twelve lines of each stanza, and each stanza is a pattern or form in which the law of sequence leads to the substitution of the leading and other terminations in a regular and pleasing order. If the order of the previous stanza be 1............12, that of the stanza in question is 11, 1, 12, 11, 2, 12, 11, 5, 5, 12, 8, 9. In each stanza the terminals of the 1st, 3d, 4th, 6th, 7th, and 10th lines are the same, and are determined by the termination of the last line of the previous stanza. The terminations of the 8th and 9th, and also of the 11th and 12th lines are the same. The form may be concisely shown by assigning the letters A B C D E to the terminations:—

1. A B A A C A A D D A E E
2. E A E E B E E C C E D D
3. D E D D A D D B B D C C
4. C D C C E C C A A C B B
5. B C B B D B B E E B A A
6. A E D D C B

Beginning at the right hand bottom corner and following the lines upwards, the letters will be found to range in alphabetical order. This system returns into itself after five variations.

Although Petrarch has left a good many sestine, subject to the above complications, yet both he and Dante, in their nobler *Canzoni*, throw off the trammels thus imposed on them. They also use the *ballata* of the Provençals, but not with its condition of being sung dancing; nor do they adopt the various repetitions (*springate*, from *springare*, to jog the feet), accompanied by various motions of the body; nor the *ritornelli*, or burdens of the song, which are repeated at intervals or at the close. Several ballata are given by Boccacio in the *Decameron*. Some of the *ballate* are named *maggiolate*, from being much in use in the month of May. There were also *serventesi*, a kind of satirical poetry, in various metres and orders of rhyme, so incatenated that a rhyme of the preceding tercet or quatrain is brought into the succeeding one. In this way arose the ordinary *terza rima*.[1]

It seems impossible to examine the forms of the Provençal poems without feeling that the sonnet is quite in harmony with them. The arrangement into quatrains, with their limited rhymes in a prescribed order, and the somewhat greater freedom in the tercets, are precisely the conditions that would meet the approval of the Provençal critic. The sonnet passed through many changes, in the length of the verses, the order of the rhymes, the addition of tails or *rondellos*; but there is no doubt that the regular sonnet of fourteen lines, with the rhymes as in Type III., was in use as early as 1321, such

---

[1] Specimens of the *Sestina*, *Madrigal*, and *Ballata*, are given in the APPENDIX.

a sonnet being written by Guglielmo de gli Amalricchi, in honour of Robert, King of Naples. In Italy, the sonnet, in the hands of Fra Guittone d'Arezzo, Dante, Cino, and lastly Petrarch, was perfected; and it seems probable that these great masters received from the Provençal poets the form of the sonnet as well as that of the *canzone*, the *sestina*, the *ballata*, etc.

The place of the sonnet in poetry thus becomes peculiar. It is the only remnant of the Provençal poets that has survived in modern song in the form and with the conditions imposed upon it by its authors. Other forms of lyric poetry have indeed come to us from the Provençals, but before adopting them they were released from most of their shackles, so as to leave the poet a large amount of freedom. The sonnet, from its brevity, its happy structure, and the facility with which it adapted itself to the wants of the poet, either did not require, or could not submit to, such treatment. It still consists of fourteen lines, and is most successful when the laws of its structure are obeyed, and the functional uses of its various parts respected (13).

11. It is, however, proper to notice that while Crescimbeni[1] and other literary historians refer to the Provençals for models for the early Italian

---

[1] *L'Istoria della Volgar Poesia scritta da Gio. Mario Crescimbeni, Canonico di S. Maria in Cosmedin, e Custode d'Arcadia.*—*Venezia* 1731.

poetry, not only with respect to the form and the rhyme, but also to the language and the ideas, later historians maintain with much force of evidence that before the Provençals even began to write, the Italians had their own language and a considerable poetical literature.[1] It is even maintained that, so far from the Italians borrowing from the Provençals, they were indebted to the Italian troubadours for their own literature.

The main points of the argument from the Italian point of view may be thus stated:—

At the time when the Provençals began to write, the Italians were in possession of their own language, which they must have abandoned had they adopted the poetry of the Provençals. In the Vatican library is a manuscript collection (Codex 3793) of the oldest and most authentic poems of the Italian troubadours. It is written on parchment, in folio, in a neat hand, and is in good preservation. The writing is of about 1265-1275. The poems are not divided into lines and stanzas, but are written like prose. The Codex contains poems by no less than one hundred Italian troubadours, all anterior to the time of Lapo, Cino, Guido, and Dante. The collection is so considerable that

---

[1] "*La lingua Italiana antichissima di origine, era gia formata e colta, quando non esisteva ancora il provenzale.*"—See *Poesie Italiane inedite di dugento autori dall' origine della lingua infino al secolo decimosettimo. Raccolte e illustrate da F. Trucchi.*—Prato, 1846.

it would occupy several thousand pages of print in octavo.

Nor can it be maintained that this codex contains all the works of the Italian troubadours, although it exceeds in bulk the whole body of Provençal poetry that has been preserved. Its style is often admirable, proving that the language must have been long cultivated, so as to have assumed a definite form in the first half of the tenth century, when many of the writers are known to have flourished.

Dante[1] and Petrarch[2] affirm that Italian poetry had its birth in Sicily. Signor Trucchi, in following up this idea, shows that the Italians, having frequent relations with the Arabs in Sicily and the Levant, borrowed from their literature and imitated their verses. Sicily was overrun by the Arabs, A.D. 820; and Palermo was captured by them in 920; and they occupied the whole island, established a stable form of government, and caused agriculture, commerce, industry, arts, and letters to flourish. In the earliest known productions of the Italian troubadours, the form, style, and modes of thought of the Arabian poets are to be traced. Like them, they accompanied their poems with music, adopting a simple and expressive melody. Hence arose the musical names of Italian poems, from *suono, tono, melodia, sonetto, canzone,* and *ballata,* as pointed out by Dante. The Court of William II., King of

---

[1] *Libro della volgar eloquenza.*   [2] *Trionfo d'Amore.*

Sicily, who ascended the throne in 1166, was the centre of the Italian troubadour's art.

It is further shown that while the Italian troubadours were constantly improving the style and range of their compositions, until they culminated in Dante and Petrarch, the Provençal poetry did not advance. That whereas the Italian troubadour was a literary man, the Provençal was a vagabond, who made a trade of his minstrelsy, and found in the manners and customs of the time abundant material for his amatory and even licentious muse, and in military exploits material for lauding the powerful. Thus, with his lute across his back, he travelled from city to city, from castle to castle, singing his verses, and attracting attention by various drolleries and buffooneries, strange dresses, and whimsical attire; thinking of anything rather than the elevating influence of good poetry on taste and morals. The Italian troubadour did think on these things; and while he of Provence and France became the jest of the common people, his Italian prototype was regarded as a teacher as well as an entertainer.

But there is proof that some of the Provençal writings are of earlier date than the Italian. On the hypothesis that the Provençals derived their poetry from the Italian, it is argued that, when, in the course of political changes, Provence became suddenly separated from that great onward movement which gained for Italy civil and political liberty, Provence became isolated and stationary, and made no advance in culture. Its language continued to be the same in the thirteenth and fourteenth centuries as in the tenth. Italy, on the contrary, during this period, was progressing in civilisation, culture, court life, university life, and republican institutions, and produced her Dante, Petrarch, Boccacio, Macchiavelli, Guicciardini, Tasso, and other men who are still dear to literature; while the works of the Provençals were completely forgotten. And although, in later times, passages from the Provençal poetry placed by the side of certain passages from Cino, Guido, Dante, and Petrarch, show a resemblance, it is contended (i.) that if those great writers imitated at all, they would not do so from a literature that they despised, but from their own early troubadours; (ii.) that the Provençals had already borrowed from the Italian troubadours poems which were known in the time of Dante and Petrarch, but subsequently lost; (iii.) that supposing there are certain passages in Petrarch, etc., which resemble those of Provençal poets, it must be remembered that the language of poetry, produced under the same conditions, has certain points of resemblance among nations that are in many respects alike; but if one nation attains to high political advantages, which the other does not realise, the literature of the one will display progress, while that of the other will remain stationary or decline. The poetical forms, sentiments, and expressions of Cino, Guido, Dante, and Petrarch, had long been in the heart and mind of the Italian people, and they had been trained thereto by the gradually increasing culture of the early Italian troubadours; and it must be added that, judging from the numerous specimens given in the volumes referred to, the Italian troubadours gained a much higher poetical footing than was ever achieved by the Provençals.

According to Signor Trucchi, rhyme, verse, and the sonnet, were spontaneous productions of the Italian language. Rhyme probably originated in the facility with which Italian words re-echo each other in similar sounds, and in the fondness of the common people for small bits of wisdom thus made to jingle. Many such of very early date are in existence, such as

Uomo che ode, vede e tace
Si vuol vivere in pace.

(He who would live in peace
Must hear, see, and from talking cease.)

Two lines or motets united in this way were called *cobbole* or *cobboletti;* Spanish, *cobla;* Provençal, *coblas;* French, *couplet* or *stanza;* and the number of lines varied from two to fifteen. A long string of motets formed a *frotta* or *frottola*, and was made in one of two ways. The frotta of two or three lines rhymed together and stood alone, this being the oldest method;

or they were worked together, so that one verse was connected with another by means of rhyme. This sort of poetry became popular in the thirteenth century, and occupied many minds in its composition. Those who made the verses also supplied the tunes to which they were sung; until, as the poetical art improved, some of the best writers preferred to call in the aid of musicians more skilled than themselves, and this led to the separation of the two arts. In the Vatican Codex is a *ballata* beginning *Lontana dimoranza*, by the troubadour Lemmi da Pistoia, under which is inscribed *Casella diede il suono;* that is, arranged the musical notes.

In the course of time the term *suono* or *sonetto* was applied to every kind of lyric poetry that was accompanied by music, and composed of stanzas united together by corresponding rhymes. The number of lines was not limited, for we have sonnets of 9, 11, 12, 16, 17, 18, and 20 lines, to say nothing of sonnets with various additions. The lines were also of different lengths, as in the following, from the Codex referred to:—

Un sonetto vollio fare *Che amorosa*
Per laudare *Bella gio mi fa provare.*
La mia donna graziosa,

(A sonnet I would write, to the praise of my gracious lady fair, whose loving care, gives true delight to me always.)

Among the specimens of the Italian troubadours

are sonnets of fourteen lines, consisting of two quatrains and two tercets, the quatrains in alternate rhyme; but when we come to what Signor Trucchi names the *Trovatori della transizione*, the sonnet begins to assume the regular form. A large number of sonnets by authors of the transition-period are given, and these are marked by elevation of thought, freshness of idea, and nobility of language, —qualities which served worthily to introduce the new school of poetry. The first regular sonnet seems to bear date somewhat anterior to 1266. After 1294 the last Italian troubadour expended himself in *Fra Guittone*.

Signor Trucchi's theory seems to prove too much, for among the numerous specimens of the troubadour muse given in his four volumes, I have not met with some of the rhythmical and metrical arrangements claimed by the Provençals. The Italian troubadour poetry is more simply constructed than theirs. I have not found among the numerous specimens given a single example of the *sestina*, the invention of which is distinctly claimed by a well-known Provençal poet, Arnaud Daniel, whose life, together with the lives of other Provençal poets, forms the subject of one of Crescimbeni's quarto volumes; so that the Provençals were not all vagabonds, but were in many cases the representatives of the literature of their time. Moreover, Signor Trucchi's theory has not been altogether accepted by Italian writers of repute. Nannucci, for example,[1] in his copious selections from the Italian troubadours, is constantly referring in his notes to words adopted by them from the Provençals. Indeed, he has a separate work entitled "Words and Phrases derived from the Provençal Language." Lastly, if the *sestina* and some other forms made use of by Dante and Petrarch are not found in the works of the Italian troubadours, but are found in those of the Provençal poets, then the conclusion must be that the Provençals invented these forms, and that Dante, Petrarch, etc., borrowed from them. Some examples of this in the case of Petrarch are given farther on (34).

But while the troubadours and the Provençals must be regarded as the representatives of the poetical mind of the time, there was another class of men who really were vagabonds of no great repute, namely, the *jongleurs* or itinerant singers, known over the greater part of Europe. The Italian *jongleurs* are noticed by Petrarch in one of his letters to Boccacio, written in 1364. He says:—" These people have not much intelligence, but a good memory and plenty of effrontery and impudence. Having nothing of their own, they plunder other people, and visit the courts of princes to declaim with much emphasis verses in the vulgar tongue

[1] *Manuale della Letteratura del primo secolo della lingua Italiana.*—*Firenze*, 1856.

which they have learnt by heart. They thus conciliate the good graces of noblemen, and get from them not only money but clothes and presents of all kinds. They replenish their stock-in-trade at the houses of the best authors, from whom they obtain verses by means of prayers, and sometimes money, should the author be needy or avaricious. I have often been importuned by them; although they come but rarely now, perhaps on account of my age, or my change of literary pursuit, or my frequent refusals,—for having often been much pestered by them I treated them with rigour, and they found me inflexible. Sometimes, however, touched by their misery or their humility, I have yielded, and employed a few hours in composing something to enable them to live. Having obtained what they wanted, I have seen them depart naked and miserable, and return some time after clad in silk, with a well-filled purse, to thank me for having drawn them out of misery. This so affected me, that considering what I did for them was in the way of alms, I was in the habit for some time of yielding to their request; but they annoyed me so often that I had to change my mode of dealing with them.

"I asked them one day why they always came to me, why they did not go to other poets,—to Boccacio, for example. They said they had often done so, and always without success. On my expressing surprise that a man so prodigal with his money should be stingy with his verses, they said that Boccacio had burnt all the verses he had made in the vulgar tongue. More surprised than before, I asked the reason. They did not know, but one of them remarked that Boccacio was waiting for time to mature his powers, in order to correct the productions of his youth. 'But why burn them,' said I, 'if he wishes to correct them?'" Petrarch knew the real reason, namely, that Boccacio, finding Petrarch's verses so superior to his own, destroyed them in a fit of discouragement. The remainder of Petrarch's letter is made up of gentle and affectionate remonstrance. "If you cannot hold the first place with Dante, why not be content with the second or the third?"

12. Whatever difficulties there may be in the way of a clear history of the origin of the sonnet, there is no doubt that it was brought to perfection by the great Italian poets, and received its highest finish from the hands of Dante and Petrarch. In proceeding to an examination of the object and purpose of the regular Italian sonnet, my illustrations will be taken chiefly from Petrarch, whose fame rests upon his sonnets and canzoni, as that of Dante upon his great epic.

The object of the regular or legitimate Italian sonnet[1] is to express one, and only one idea, mood,

---

[1] The term regular, or legitimate, is applied to the sonnet of fourteen lines, the structure of which has been already explained (1)

sentiment, or proposition, and this must be introduced in appropriate language in the first quatrain, and so far explained in the second, that this may end in a full point; while the office of the first tercet is to prepare the leading idea of the quatrains for the conclusion, which conclusion is to be perfectly carried out in the second tercet, so that it may contain the fundamental idea of the poem, and end, as it were, with the point of an epigram. In short, the quatrains should contain the proposition and proof; the tercets its confirmation and conclusion. It must be obvious that such conditions exclude the final couplet of the English sonnet, and are also opposed to the practice so common with Wordsworth and other celebrated English sonnet-writers, of running the second quatrain into the first tercet. If the English had followed the Italian practice of printing the sonnet—that is,

(2) (3). It excludes such odd and fanciful varieties as *caudated* or *tailed sonnets; mute sonnets*, in which the rhymes are of one syllable, as in English, although in Italian this form is limited to comic subjects; *iterating* or *continuous sonnets*, in which only one or two words are used to end every line, as in Petrarch's sixteenth sonnet,—the terminal words, instead of rhyming, are reiterated, thus:—

Parte,	*luce,*	*luce,*	*parte.*
Parte,	*luce,*	*luce,*	*parte.*
Morte,	*desio,*	*sole.*	
Morte,	*desio,*	*sole.*	

There are also *retrograde sonnets*, which read the same forwards and backwards; *chained* or *linked sonnets*, in which each successive verse derives at least one of its rhymes from the preceding stanza; *interwoven sonnets*, in which words rhyme in the middle of the lines as well as at the end; and some others.

with such an arrangement of type as to distinguish each separate part, and show that it really is a structure made up of four distinct members or organs—the defect alluded to would probably have corrected itself by the eye as well as by the ear. It must, however, be confessed that the sonnet is much better adapted to the Italian language than to the English tongue; for, whereas, the former contains such a wealth of disyllabic rhymes, that there is no difficulty whatever in limiting the sonnet to four or at most five flowing rhymed endings, our rhymes being mostly monosyllabic, greatly limit our power of rhyming. Moreover, the mode of reading Italian poetry, so as to secure the rhythm, is different from our own, and this gives a much greater facility of expression to the Italian. As Italian words, with very few exceptions, terminate in vowels, the final vowel is cut off before a word beginning with a vowel; so that the usual line of eleven syllables may really be extended to thirteen or more, and yet be read only as a five feet line. Thus, in the 313th sonnet of Petrarch the first line of the second quatrain—

"*Tu, che vedi i miei mali indegni ed empi,*"

contains sixteen syllables, so that in reading the line three elisions have to be made.[1] In the hands

---

[1] According to Dryden (Dedication prefixed to the second volume of the translation of Virgil, 1730), the language is made of such soft metal as to require an alloy of this kind, to give it sufficient

of a good poet a line may thus be produced so pregnant with meaning that it cannot be properly rendered into an English heroic verse, which can claim no such privilege as that of the Italian. I do not know how the above line, for example, is to be translated into a corresponding English line, so as to give the sense and yet be rhythmical. Happily, Petrarch's verses are not always so full of meaning as this; on the contrary, they are often so diffuse, that the difficulty lies the other way, the English being more terse than the Italian; so that it often requires padding, or the feeble aid of expletives, to make up the full measure of the verse. This remark, however, does not apply to the sonnet above referred to, which is full of condensed thought pathetically and even majestically expressed,—so much so, that some critics, English and Italian, refer to it as the finest of Petrarch's sonnets. In order that the reader may form his own judgment, I append the sonnet in the original, and also an attempt to render it into English with the same metrical arrangement.[1]

hardness for coining, that is, for good writing. Nevertheless, this extensive cutting off of the vowels is a great advantage to the author, and sometimes an equally great disadvantage to the translator.

[1] A friend of mine, who translated this sonnet, has allowed me to improve my translation by a reference to his; and he is so good as to say that he has improved his by a reference to mine. I am also indebted to him for taking the trouble to revise most of the translations contained in this volume.

Sonetto CCCXIII.—Type II.

I'vo piangendo i miei passati tempi,
I quai posi in amar cosa mortale,
Senza levarmi a volo, avend 'io l'ale,
Per dar forse di me non bassi esempi.
Tu, che vedi i miei mali indegni ed empi,
Re del Cielo, invisibile, immortale,
Soccorri all' alma disviata e frale,
E'l suo difetto di tua grazia adempi.
Si che, s' io vissi in guerra ed in tempesta,
Mora in pace ed in porto; e se la stanza
Fu vana, almen sia la partita onesta.
A quel poco di viver, che m' avanza,
Ed al morir degni esser tua man presta:
Tu sai ben che 'n altrui non ho speranza.

Translation.

I still lament, with tears, the years gone by,
  Wasted in loving but a mortal thing;
  Though I could soar, not rising on the wing,
  To lofty work, which might perchance not die.
O Thou! who knowest my impiety,
  Invisible, immortal, heavenly King!
  To my frail wand'ring soul some succour bring,
  And its defects of Thy own grace supply.
Though tempest-toss'd and oft in strife I be,
  At peace, in port, let me my life resign,
  Though spent in vain, yet close in piety:
In that short span of life I yet call mine,
  And in death's hour extend Thy hand to me;
  Thou know'st I trust no other aid but Thine.

13. Now the question is, whether this is a perfect sonnet: that is, does it fulfil all the conditions required by the great Italian masters and critics in this class of composition? and these conditions are sufficiently comprehensive and stringent. In the first place, the quatrains must not contain more than two, nor the tercets more than three, rhymes. (ii.) The rhymes must be sufficiently varied and contrasted without being forced, and must fall into their places so naturally as never to suggest the idea that a word, much less a line, is introduced for the sake of the rhyme. The contrast of rhymes just referred to, must be observed not only with respect to the two rhymes of the quatrains, but these must be in contrast with the two or three rhymes of the tercets; that is, the contrasted rhymes must not play upon the same vowel. For example, either of the following would be a bad set of rhymes for a quatrain, because in each case the four words depend upon the same vowel:—

    time, side, wide, chime,
or   way, gain, remain, day.

(iii.) The sonnet must consist of one leading idea, or thought or feeling. (iv.) The words employed must be choice and effective—no word must be out of place, and there must not be a word too much or too little.[1] (v.) The thought must be worked out

---

[1] Leigh Hunt (*Book of the Sonnet*) says it is better to avoid

with perfect clearness; there must be no obscurity of meaning, no sense of irrelevancy or insufficiency; but the poem must go on increasing in interest and lead up to an impressive close. (vi.) It must further be noted that the second quatrain should not be run into the first tercet, but close with a full point; and the sonnet must not end with a couplet, nor with an Alexandrine.

Does the sonnet before us comply with these conditions? (i.) There are only two rhymes in the quatrains and only two in the tercets. (ii.) The rhymes in the quatrains are sufficiently varied, *empi* and *ale* employing different vowels; while in the tercets *esta* and *anza* are sufficiently removed from each other, and from the terminations in the quatrains. (iii.) The idea is clear and distinct—the poet laments his wasted years and follies, and prays for pardon and peace at the last. (iv.) The words employed are choice and expressive; although the commentator Tassoni objects somewhat to the expression *porre i tempi*, " to place one's times," instead of *spendere il tempo*, " to spend one's time;" and both he and Muratori object that *vana* and *onesta* in

---

the use of long words, as they tend to diminish the number of accents, and thus weaken the verse. This cannot be said to apply to the Italian sonnet. Dante uses long words with good effect, as, for example—
Passa una donna baldanzosamente,
and Cino—
Com' sta tra voi maravigliosamente.

the first tercet are not properly antithetical. (v.) The thought is worked out with perfect clearness, although, according to Muratori, not altogether with perfect dignity of expression. As to the sixth condition, this is never transgressed by the best Italian sonnet writers.

The conclusion is, that this sonnet, if not quite perfect, is very nearly so, the flaws pointed out being so very minute as to require for their detection the microscope of the professional commentator. As to the translation, I cannot say that it satisfies me, and it may be doubted whether any translation can satisfy a correct taste based on a proper estimation of the poetry of the original. The difficulties of the translator's task can only be appreciated by the reader becoming the translator. Let any one try his hand at a sonnet by one of the Italian masters, with the firm determination not to introduce any ideas of his own, not a word but what is strictly sanctioned by the original, and he will undertake a wholesome task as regards his own culture, although his candour must soon compel him to admit that it is a difficult one. If Wordsworth confessed himself baffled in the attempt to translate the sonnets of Michael Angelo,[1] that fact ought to

---

[1] "So much meaning has been put by Michael Angelo into so little room, and that meaning sometimes so excellent in itself, that I found the difficulty of translating him insurmountable. I attempted, at least, fifteen of the sonnets, but could not anywhere succeed. I have sent you the only one I was able to finish; it is

teach smaller men modesty. There is, however, this excuse for our laureate, that he worked on a vitiated text. Michael Angelo did not publish his sonnets during his life; after his death his great-nephew took possession of his papers, and fancied he could improve upon these famous productions. The natural result was that he frequently injured them by substituting his own weak language for the thunder tones of his uncle, and by rendering obscure many passages that were before clear. We owe a debt of gratitude to Signor Quasti, who, in 1863, collated the published poems with the original MSS., and for the first time gave these fine productions to the world in the language of their great author.

In order that we may become more fully impressed with the conditions required in the production of a sonnet of the highest order, such as the one just quoted, I proceed to notice one of Petrarch's failures, remarking, however, that such a failure might pass for the success of an inferior poet. In order to the better understanding of the criticism, the original accompanies the translation.

far from being the best or most characteristic, but the others were too much for me."—*Life of Wordsworth.*

Sonetto CCXXXI.—Type I.

La vita fugge, e non s'arresta un 'ora;
  E la morte vien dietro a gran giornate;
  E le cose presenti, e le passate
  Mi danno guerra, e le future ancora;
E'l rimembrar, e l'aspettar m'accora
  Or quinci, or quindi si, che 'n veritate,
  Se non ch' i 'ho di me stesso pietate,
  I' sarei già di questi pensier fora.
Tornami avanti, s'alcun dolce mai
  Ebbe 'l cor tristo; e poi dall 'altra parte
  Veggio al mio navigar turbati i venti:
Veggio fortuna in porto; e stanco omai
  Il mio nocchier; e rotte arbore, e sarte;
  E i lumi bei, che mirar soglio, spenti.

Translation.

Life hurries on without an hour's delay,
  And Death, with eager step, pursuing goes;
  The present and the past give no repose,
  And the dread future fills me with dismay.
Rememb'ring or expecting, every way
  I turn, so whelms my heart with woes,
  If pity to myself did not oppose,
  I were from all these thoughts long since away.
Hither I ask if aught of sweetness went
  To visit the sad heart. Without avail
  Thither I strive against the storm's fierce breath.
But storms I see in port; and tempest-spent
  My pilot, rent my masts, torn every sail,
  And the sweet eyes I love now quenched in death.

This sonnet opens with a striking metaphor, which, however, is not sustained. Life hurrying on its journey, closely pursued by death, is first made a matter of complaint; the metaphor is then changed into a tempest-battered ship, which the prevailing storm excludes from the port [of old age or death], and this is made a matter of regret. Thus the opening and the close, though each finely told, and the last line exquisite, do not blend, and are not in harmony with each other, or with the middle portion. This middle portion displays a poverty both of material and of language in the third, fourth, fifth, and sixth lines. The poet seems to have been labouring under a strong attack of prose, or he would not have employed such commonplace expressions as the following:—

E le cose presenti, e le passate,

"things present and past," in the third line, and

Or quinci, or quindi si, che 'n veritate,

"this way or that way, so that in truth," in the sixth. Moreover, the ideas expressed by these commonplace lines are repeated in the tercets. Hence, we conclude, that although this sonnet is unobjectionable in mechanical structure, and contains some exquisite poetry, it cannot take rank as a first-rate sonnet, because it fails to comply with the conditions (iii.), (iv.), and (v.)

If, in the foregoing sonnet, there is a confusion

of metaphor, the reader will find that in the following the metaphor is well sustained:—

SONNET CLVI.
TYPE I. } *Passa la nave mia colma d'obblio.*

My ship, oblivion-laden, o'er the sea,
   O'er the rough sea, 'neath midnight wintry sky,
   'Twixt Scylla and Charyb, Love makes to fly,
For at the helm sits he, mine enemy.
Some bold, dark thought, seems at each oar to be,
   Which scorns the tempest, laughs though Death be nigh;
   A ceaseless gale, suffused with many a sigh,
Desire and hope, the sail rends fearfully.
A shower of tears, a cloud too of disdain,
   Both bathes and slackens the much-wearied cords,
   With ignorance and error intertwined:
My wonted guides, twin stars, concealed remain;
   Reason or art, storm-spent, no aid affords;
   I almost fear the port I may not find.

14. Some of our best English sonnets end with a long line or Alexandrine, and also with a rhymed couplet. No example of either practice occurs in the Italian sonnet. The long line is not wanted, because, from the mode of reading Italian verse, the poet can condense as much or as little thought into one line as suits his purpose. The rhymed couplet at the end, in addition to the one in each quatrain, would probably offend the sensitive ear of the Italian poet or reader; and a more serious objection

is, that it would destroy the tercets, and convert the sonnet into something else not intended by the great Masters. Hence it is opposed to the Italian form, even when the opportunity for introducing it seems tempting; and, according to our English notions, would be an appropriate mode of winding up the argument. The following is an example of this, taken from the occasional sonnets. It is addressed to the famous Captain Pandolfo Malatesta, lord of Rimini.[1]

SONNET LXXXIII. { *L'aspettata virtù, che 'n voi fioriva.*

The budding virtues that appeared in thee,
   When Love first sought to bring thee 'neath his power,
   Now bear a fruit well worthy of the flower,
And my best hopes all realised I see.
Therefore, my heart suggests the thought to me,
   To write thy deeds, so that thy fame may soar;
   The sculptor's art is feeble to secure
To his skilled marble immortality.

Think you that Cæsar, or Marcellus lives,
   Or Paul or Africanus finds his fame,
In works the anvil or the mallet gives?
   Time's finger doth their feebleness proclaim.
But oh! my friend! the poet's art sublime
To men gives fame, that scorns the touch of time.

---

[1] This sonnet formed the subject of a lecture by Bonsi, delivered before the Florentine Academy on the 6th July 1549. He points out that the Paul referred to in the sonnet is Paulus Æmilius the younger.

If the reader will take the trouble to compare this version with the original, he will find that it offends against the principle of the sonnet. In the original the tercets are quite distinct, and each tercet has its appropriate function.

> *Credete voi che Cesare, o Marcello,*
>   *O Paolo, od African fossin cotali*
>   *Per incude giammai, ne per martello?*
> *Pandolfo mio, quest 'opere son frali*
>   *Al lungo andar; ma 'l nostro studio è quello*
>   *Che fa per fama gli uomini immortali.*

> Think you that Cæsar, or Marcellus,
>   Or Paul, or Africanus, were such [*i.e.* immortal]
>   Through any work of anvil or of mallet?
> O my Pandolf! these works are frail
>   In the long run; but our art is that
>   Which makes men immortal through fame.

The leading idea of this sonnet naturally assumes the syllogistic form, thus :—

That which confers lasting fame ought to endure for ever.
The work of the poet lasts for ever.
Hence we conclude that the work of the poet confers lasting fame.

Or again :—

That which confers lasting fame ought to endure for ever.
The work of the sculptor does not endure for ever.
∴ The work of the sculptor does not confer lasting fame.

If the sonnet be capable of this logical treatment, it becomes doubly important that its several parts be kept quite distinct, and not be run into each other.

I do not maintain that all the best sonnets invariably admit of this dry analysis; but the possibility of such an analysis is among the conditions of success, and success greatly depends upon an accurate knowledge of the conditions.

15. The best sonnets of Petrarch are included under one or other of the three types already noted: those that are inferior have an awkward, straggling distribution of the tercets. Some of the sonnets are disfigured by conceits and metaphysical subtleties, which, however, are not very numerous, considering the early period of the compositions, their devotion, for the most part, to one object, extending over a period of two-and-thirty years, and the powerful example of the troubadour lyrics, which were formerly sung over Europe. Poems, thus limited, naturally repeat the same thought, and often recur to the same idea. It would be too much to expect that the lady's name of Laura should not tempt the poet to play upon the word and ring changes with it, and with *Laura* "the laurel," and *l'aura* "the gentle gale," as when *l'aura move il verdi lauro;* and curiously enough, in the early printed copies (the first is dated 1472), mistakes arose between *Laura* the lady's name and *l'aura* the gale, from the

circumstance that the early printers had not yet invented the apostrophe, so that if a compositor omitted a space between the article and the noun, *L'aura* would read *Laura*. So also in the fifth sonnet *Quand io move*, etc., a play on Laura's name, LAU-RE-TA is made to teach LAUdare, REverire and TAcere—to praise—to revere—and to be silent. The sixth sonnet, *Si traviato*, etc., is a beautiful production, but in the last tercet the poet is again caught in the snare of a bad pun. Another figure turning on the word *keys* is similarly twisted into various shapes. Thus Laura keeps the *keys* of his heart; or has in her hand either *key;* she herself is the *key;* her eyes are *keys;* amorous *keys*, and so on. Then again Laura is the *sun*, her countenance is a *sun*, her person a *sun*, her eyes are *suns*, her hair a *sun*. In the 217th sonnet, *La sera desia*, etc., heaven is enamoured of the earth on account of Laura, not less than the earth is enamoured of heaven on account of the sun. If the sun rise before Laura he is very bright, but as soon as Laura gets up, his lustre becomes dimmed.[1] We may excuse these occasional extravagances on the part of a great poet, on the ground that they are occasional, while the bulk of his work consists of true poetry. Unfortunately Petrarch's imitators (and their name is

---

[1] De Sade, in quoting an Italian writer who admired this rivalry of the two suns, says, "Je doute que ce *concetto* fasse fortune en France."

legion) do not give us true poetry, but do give the bombast: and they seem to have drawn so largely on the sun, as to justify the complaint of Salvator Rosa, in one of his satires, that "these metaphors had exhausted the sun."

16. It is commonly supposed that Petrarch is the inventor of that kind of amatory poetry which exalts itself and its object without depending on the passions, except so far as love must, more or less, have the character of a human passion. But, as Fraticelli remarks, Petrarch found the language enriched, refined, and made acceptable, both to the common people and to the learned, by the works of Dante, whose sonnets are entirely free from the defects just pointed out. To Petrarch is due the merit not only of producing a large amount of exquisite poetry, but of carrying the language to the highest perfection. It is easy to magnify the defects of this poetry so as to obscure its beauties; but the real merit of Petrarch, as the author above referred to well remarks, is in being natural, and then we recognise in him the same qualities that enchant us in Dante, that inspiration of deep and ardent affection, that elevation of thought and delicacy of sentiment, polished language, magnificent style, and, above all, that spirit of self-sacrifice with which he inspires the reader, whereby he ennobles love, and sacrifices himself and his passion to the beloved object and to virtue.

17. The story of Petrarch and Laura has often been told; and has furnished a literary problem to many a critic. Several theories have been started respecting Laura :—(i.) That she was an ideal creation of the poet, destined to stimulate his muse; (ii.) That she personified virtue, science, or philosophy; (iii.) That, under the disguise of Laura, the poet really worshipped the Virgin Mary. Even during the lifetime of the poet, one of his most intimate friends, the Bishop of Lombes, wrote to him in 1335 :— " Your Laura is but a phantom, created by your imagination, as a subject whereon to exercise your muse and procure you a name. Your verses, your love, your sighs, only deal in fiction, and if they contain anything real, it is your passion, not for Laura, who exists only in your imagination, but for the laurel with which poets are crowned. This is the object of your ambition, as all your works prove."

The latter part of the charge was true, for Petrarch did covet the laurel crown, and received it at Rome in 1341, at the instance of that enlightened sovereign, Robert of Naples. As to the former part of the charge the good Bishop was mistaken, as we know from the abundant evidence collected by the Abbé de Sade and the internal evidence of Petrarch's writings, among which may be cited the poet's reply to his friend's bantering letter. He says—" Would to heaven that my Laura were an imaginary personage, and that my passion for her were only a pastime. Alas! it is a frenzy, and although it would be difficult and painful to feign long, it would be extravagance to play such a comedy. One can mimic the sick man in action, voice, and gestures, but one cannot assume his air and pallor. How often have you witnessed my pale cheek and my torments? . . . You exhort me to love you. Alas! in matters of love, I have more need of the bridle than the spur, and I should be more tranquil had I not so tender a heart."

The Bishop had some excuse for supposing Laura to have been a creation of the poet, in the fact that Dante and his friends were accustomed to address imaginary as well as real beauties, and it is not always easy to distinguish one from the other. There is no doubt that Dante's Beatrice was as real a person as Petrarch's Laura; but Dante often identified his love of Beatrice with his love of philosophy, and even addressed the latter in passionate terms, such as might readily be mistaken for the ardent outpourings of a tender lover. It is quite necessary to understand this, otherwise the lyric poetry of Dante would be often unintelligible. In the first of the following sonnets, for example, the two ladies in question are, the one Beatrice, and the other philosophy; the one sensual and the other intellectual love. In the second sonnet, the lady seems to be philosophy alone, whom in the *Convito* (iii. 10) he calls disdainful, proud, and cruel; because although he courted her with the assiduity of a lover she did not reward him even with a smile; but remained cold, hard, and difficult.

SONNET XLII. } *Due Donne in cima della mente*
TYPE II.   }   *mia.*

Two ladies in my intellect's high seat,
   To hold discourse on love are come to me.
   In one these virtues—valour, courtesy,
   Prudence and honesty together meet.[1]
Beauty the other has and charms most sweet,
   And graceful gentleness in her you see;[2]
   All thanks to my sweet lord's[3] benignity,
   I place myself a subject at their feet.
Beauty and Wisdom[4] to my reason say,
   "How can a heart be given to ladies twain,
   And yet the laws of perfect love obey?"
The fount of gentle parlance[5] makes it plain
   That love of Beauty points to bliss the way,[6]
   From love of Wisdom, we high deeds obtain.[7]

SONNET XLIII. } *Nulla mi parrà mai più crudel*
TYPE I.   }   *cosa.*

Ah! what more cruel fate than this, that she
   I serve, and serving, pine my life away,
   Her passion keeps in frozen lake alway,
   And mine condemns in love's fierce heat to be.
That wondrous beauty I may only see,

---

[1] The celestial lady, Wisdom. [2] The terrestrial lady. [3] Love.
[4] The two ladies in question.
[5] Love again. [6] Sensual love. [7] Intellectual love.

> Her cruel, cold disdain, alone survey;
> And so completely own my torment's sway,
> That other joy my eyes dare not bring me.
> The flower that turns to gaze upon the sun,
> Though ever changing, unchanged love holds dear,[1]
> Ne'er felt such cruel strokes of fate as I:
> And since she, proud, by love may not be won,
> Love sometimes visits me, my life to cheer,
> And for each sigh of mine, gives back a sigh.

18. If we compare the Laura of Petrarch with the Beatrice of Dante, as exhibited in the sonnets of the two poets, we gradually become alive to this striking difference, namely, that Laura is too exalted a being for this earth, while Beatrice is a living, loveable woman. Laura is not only transcendently beautiful, but, seen through the fervid medium of the poet's imagination, her charms have a magical influence on Nature herself. Her eyes are brighter than the sun, and her death extinguishes his splendour; her presence calms and brightens the air; she imparts to the banks of the Sorga its freshness and verdure; the flowers court the touch of her feet; and Heaven looks down upon her in wonder and admiration. All this may be the natural expression of the poet's exaggerated imagination, because the

---

[1] This may remind the reader of Moore :—
> "As the sunflower turns to her god when he sets
> The same look that she gave when he rose."

But the idea is borrowed from Ovid.—*Metam.* iv. v. 270.
> "Vertitur ad solem, mutataque servat amorem.'

love of a good woman makes even Nature herself look more beautiful; and by an easy reflex action, the cause of the heightened charms of Nature is referred to the beloved object. Such ecstacy, however, fails to give us a true picture of a living woman. On the other hand, Beatrice is not presented to us through her beauties so much as through her moral graces, and that sweet influence which a good woman exerts on all around her. The poet takes it for granted that she is beautiful, and then gives full scope to the excellences of character by which she influences others. Every one must have known a Beatrice in the course of his life; a being surrounded by a sort of moral atmosphere which diffuses goodness, so that the coarser nature of men shrinks before it, and feels as it were reproved. His heart flutters at her salute; and, conscious of his errors, he sighs when he is thus, by a sort of instinct, made to feel how great a distance there is between her purity and his coarseness. Even her own sex is made better by her presence, which bears with it a blessing; it extinguishes envy and pride, and all the evil passions quail before that miracle of gentleness. This is higher art than that of Petrarch, and is possessed by few poets. Spenser and Shakspere knew how to use it, and in modern literature Göthe's Gretchen, and a few other rare instances, are cases in point.

There is yet another difference between the sonnets of Petrarch and Dante. Petrarch's outpourings are personal to himself; they speak the language of his own heart, and although that language may be true, its vocabulary is limited, and it requires similar conditions in others before its expression can be felt and understood. This particularly applies to the sonnets of the *Vita*. In those of the *Morte* the language of bereavement is more expansive, and hence more akin to our sympathy; but even here it requires us to know what bereavement really is, before we can fully enter into the spirit of the poetry. Dante, on the other hand, is not so personal; he does not remind us of himself; but he enlists the sympathies of humanity, so that any one reading his sonnets, may feel that the poet is actually addressing him; for by his breadth of treatment he calls to mind some loved friend, living or dead, and does honour to the presence, or to the memory of some one that is, or has been, dearer to us than all the world beside.

The contrast thus pointed out cannot be better illustrated than by a sonnet from each of these masters.

LAURA.

SONNET CLIX. } *Stiamo Amor, a veder la gloria*
TYPE I. } *nostra.*

O Love! stand here, and on our glory gaze,
   Things above Nature towering new and fair;

Mark well in her those showers of sweetness rare,
   And light that Heaven alone on earth displays.
What art adorns those charms above all praise
   In purple, pearls and gold, not seen elsewhere:
   How sweet her feet and glancing eyes appear,
   In the dark cloister these loved hills upraise,
Flowers of a thousand tints, the herbage green,
   Beneath this ancient sombre oak outspread,
   Are emulous to touch her lovely feet;
While, in the sky, bright sailing clouds are seen
   Kindled by her, as if in joy, they said:—
   " Those lustrous eyes make Nature calm and sweet."[1]

BEATRICE.

SONNET XIX.
1 2 1 2, 1 2 1 2 } *Di donne io vidi una gentile schiera.*
3 4 3, 4 3 4.

It was on All Saints' Day that's just gone by,
   I saw some ladies pass, a gentle band,
   And she who chief seemed of that company
Came forward, leading Love on her right hand.
Her eyes shone forth with so much brilliancy,
   As of a spirit from celestial land;

---

[1] Ugo Foscolo, in his *Essays on Petrarch* (London, 1823), has an Essay entitled "A Parallel between Dante and Petrarch," in which he remarks with reference to this sonnet:—" This description makes us long to find such a woman in the world." It is to be noted, as a proof how little Dante's sonnets are known and appreciated, that Foscolo makes no reference to them; and Carlyle, in his lecture on Dante and Shakspere (*Hero Worship*, Lecture III.), exhibits the same abstinence; although, in referring to Shakspere, he remarks that "these sonnets of his will even testify expressly in what deep waters he had waded and swam, struggling for his life." Dante's great poem seems to have eclipsed his minor poems.

And as I gazed with more persistency,
An angel seemed before my sight to stand.
On him who's worthy, meekly she bestowed
Her salutation, with a look benign;
So that his heart with goodness overflowed;
She surely comes from heaven—a thing divine,
And, for our good, on earth has her abode;
So blest is he who near her may remain.

19. In examining a tabulated list of Petrarch's sonnets, in metrical arrangement, according to types and other similar lists which I have made of the sonnets of Dante, Tasso, Ariosto, Michael Angelo, and Vittoria Colonna, it is found that several sonnets under the same type follow in consecutive numerical order. Now we may suppose the sonnets to be arranged in the order in which they were written, and there is no reason to doubt that it is so, for in Petrarch's the occasional sonnets are mixed up in the *Vita* and the *Morte*, although they are entirely removed from the subject matter of either; and in Tasso's we know, from the events of his life, the order in which some of the principal sonnets ought to be arranged. Now, supposing this to be the case, it would seem that the production of a successful sonnet impressed on the poet's mind a kind of persistence in the same plane of motion, which led him to go on writing sonnets under the same metrical type. Among Tasso's sonnets are twelve consecutive compositions called *corone* or

coronali, forming what is called a "crown of sonnets." These belong to the same type; but there is another reason for this strict attention to method;—these twelve sonnets refer to one subject, and hence, in the hands of a poet who studied method, they would require to be arranged in the same metrical form, so as to produce a symmetrical crown for the head of the object of the laudation.

Lessons in method are given to us whenever we gain some idea of the mode in which great men accomplish their work. For example, in the autobiographical sketch known as the *Vita Nuova*, or "new" or "youthful life" of Dante, which contains some of his very best sonnets (or, in other words, perfect models of this class of composition), the poet not only gives an account of the origin of each particular sonnet, but, in some cases, sets it out fully in his prose narrative, then gives the sonnet itself, and not content with this, appends a kind of gloss or interpretation of the poem. In the following sonnet—

Vede perfettamente ogni salute,

a full account is given of its origin, which I shall have occasion to quote further on (21); but I give here a translation of the sonnet and of the gloss, for the purpose of showing that so lofty a genius as Dante did not shrink from hard work in order to produce good results.

Sonnet XVIII. } *Vede perfettamente ogni*
1 2 1 2, 1 2 1 2 } *salute.*
3 4 5, 3 4 5. }

He sees each form of goodness perfectly,
    Who, among other ladies, looks on mine;
    And her companions should, most duteously,
    For such sweet grace, in thanks, to God incline.
Such virtue in her beauty all must see,
    That envy causes no one to repine;
    But in her lustre clad, she seems to be
    Of love, and faith and gentleness, the shrine.
Her presence makes all else more meanly show,
    Her presence more than pleasure doth confer,
    For each, through her, in honour may improve.
From every act of hers such graces flow,
    That no one in his mind can image her,
    But he must sigh in all the sweets of love.

Dante's gloss on the sonnet is as follows:—

"This sonnet is divided into three parts: in the first of which, I say among what kind of people this lady appears admirable; in the second, I say how gracious was her company; in the third, I say what were the virtuous effects she produced on others. The second part commences with the line 'And her companions,' etc., the third 'Such virtue in her beauty,' etc. This last part also divides itself into three—in the first, I say what effect she had upon other ladies, that is, they following her example. In the second, I say what she produced in them through others. In the third, I say not only how she influenced other ladies, but all persons, and that not only by her presence, but thinking of her, how admirably she worked for good. The second commences thus, 'Her presence,' etc., and the the third, 'From every act of hers,' etc."

We have a still better opportunity of knowing how earnestly Petrarch laboured to make his poems as perfect as possible, from the account given by Ubaldini, in 1642, of Petrarch's manuscripts. Some of these are dotted over with annotations, which show how anxiously the author wrote and re-wrote, revised and corrected his verses; and, curiously enough, he usually devoted Friday, a day of fasting and humiliation, to the task of revision. Muratori gives a number of examples of this kind; and Ugo Foscolo, in one of his essays, translates from the Latin a series of memoranda attached to one of the sonnets to the following effect :—

"I began this by the impulse of the Lord, 10th September, at the dawn of day, after my morning prayers."

"I must re-write these two verses, singing them, and I must transpose them. 3 o'clock A.M., 19th October."

"I like this. 30th Oct., 10 o'clock in the morning."

"No! this does not please me. 20th December, in the evening."

And in the midst of his corrections he writes, on laying down his pen—

"I shall return to this; I am called to supper."

"February 18th, towards noon.—This is now well, but look at it again."

In the midst of his corrections, or even of his composition, he was in the habit of noting down a thought that suddenly occurred to him. For example—" Consider this. I had some thoughts of transposing these lines and of making the first verse the last, but I have not done so for the sake of harmony—the first would then be more sonorous, and the last less so, which is against rule; for the end should be more harmonious than the beginning."

In another place he says:—" The commencement is good, but it is not sufficiently pathetic." Every verse is turned in several different ways: above each phrase and each word are frequently placed equivalent expressions for after-examination; and Ugo Foscolo remarks that " it requires a profound knowledge of Italian to perceive that after such perplexing scruples, he always adopts those words which combine at once most harmony, elegance, and energy."

In a letter addressed to a dignitary who had sent him a number of verses written within a brief space of time, Petrarch contrasts his own practice. He says:—" The sun rises and sets, and sees me engaged on the same production. When I take pen in hand my imagination represents to me posterity as a severe judge, whose decision I have reason to fear. This makes my work proceed slowly. I pass the file over it again and again, and can scarcely make up my mind to allow it to go out of my cabinet. The courier knocks at my door, but I prefer to send him away empty rather than publish things at which I should afterwards blush. . . Could I, like you, write verses by the thousand, however good and harmonious they might appear, I would not do so, unless the rhythm were rigorously accurate, unless they had a certain poetical charm, unless they diffused a light capable of raising and edifying the mind."

We also know, from Petrarch's letters, that he often wrote to a friend details that were fresh in his mind, and which he afterwards condensed into a sonnet. It is instructive to note how in this way a page of prose becomes transformed into fourteen pregnant lines.

20. It has been suggested that if poetry be thus painfully elaborated, the passion of which it is the vehicle must be as artificial as the verse. In examining this question it must be remembered that Petrarch's Italian verses, disencumbered of the labours of the commentators, are contained in a small pocket volume of 300 pages, and consist of 317 *Sonetti*, forty-nine *Canzoni*, and seven *Trionfi*, and were spread over two-and-thirty years of a life which was often devoted to the service of his country, and required our poet not only to visit various parts of Italy but also distant States of Europe. He was naturally fond of study and the

retirement necessary for its successful prosecution, and in the intervals of these fatiguing political missions he found the solitude of the closed valley (Vaucluse) refreshing. He gives several descriptions of his mode of life in this solitude. In one of them he says—" I rise at midnight—I go out at break of day—I study in the fields as in my library—I read, I write, I dream—I struggle against indolence, luxury, and pleasure. I wander all day among the arid mountains, the fresh valleys, and the deep caverns. I walk much on the banks of the Sorga, where I meet no one to distract me—I recall the past—I deliberate on the future; and in this contemplation I find a resource against my solitude." Many of Petrarch's best sonnets were written in these intervals of leisure, and contain descriptions of the locality, and of his own varied moods of thought and feeling.[1] But he had also other employments. He devoted much time to

[1] One of Petrarch's friends thus describes the poet's life at Vaucluse :—"I picture to myself everything you do at Vaucluse in the course of the day. At sunrise, wakened by the concerts of the birds and the murmurs of your fountain, you climb the dew-clad hills, from which you look down upon the cultivated plains, and, perhaps, on the sea covered with mist. You always have your tablets in your hand to which you confide any new thought. When the sun has risen above the horizon you return to your little house to a repast like that of Curius and Fabricius, and this is succeeded by a short nap. Then to avoid the heat of the day you go into the valley so justly named Vaucluse." After describing the grotto, he proceeds :—" Here you exercise your mind in the production of those masterpieces which the Nymphs and the Muses so much applaud ; and here it is that, regarding the pomps and riches of this

the composition of his Latin works, on which he vainly hoped to build his fame. He also occupied himself in transcribing, or getting transcribed, the work of any classical author that fell in his way, and to this circumstance we are indebted for the preservation of the works of Cicero and others, which would otherwise have been lost, or have come down to us in a still more imperfect form than we now possess them.[1] A vigorous mind may suffer from a hopeless passion, or from the death of a beloved object, and express that suffering in so touching a cry that every sufferer who hears it, even after the lapse of ages, shall recognise it as the voice of nature. What though that cry be now and then disfigured by an exaggerated tone? it belongs to the quality of strong feeling to make use of strong language; but in the midst of it all the voice of suffering is the true voice to which similar suffering responds, and if Petrarch's poetry pass through the crucible of a suffering mind unscathed, then that poetry is a true expression, and not an artificial counterfeit, of grief. I contend that a considerable number of these poems respond to this test. But

---

world as a shadow that passeth away, you renounce them in order that you may usefully employ your time. When you leave this grotto, if your hands are empty your tablets are full. Do not think that the treasures of your mind are enjoyed by yourself alone; my mind, which is never absent from you, shares in this enjoyment, as useful as it is agreeable. Adieu, my dear Petrarch, and forget not another yourself."

[1] See APPENDIX.

if the poet be thus occasionally overcome by real emotion and knows how to express it, does it follow that because he is not always weeping, but with the self-denial and elasticity of a noble nature recovers himself from time to time, and turns to other pursuits,—does it follow that when he does weep his tears should be false and affected? To suppose this is to take a very narrow view of the breadth and variety of a fine mind, which, with a capacity for much suffering, has also a capacity for much enjoyment and intellectual work; and while occasionally relieving one by the other, is also capable of engaging in pursuits that bear no reference to either.

21. Still, however, in estimating Petrarch's burning language and impassioned praise as applied to Laura, and the more than angelic beauty he confers upon her, we must take into account the circumstances of the times in which he lived. He was too near the age of chivalry not to be affected by it; and chivalry exalted the being and condition of woman into something divine. Then, again, the troubadours and the courts of love had not ceased to exercise their curious functions, among which the adoration and exaltation of the fair sex were prime objects: these too had an influence. But, above all, the Platonic idea of love, which had been introduced into Italy by the Fathers of the Church, was sure to have a subtle and powerful effect on so poetical a temperament as that of

Petrarch. According to this theory, love is a strong desire for the beautiful—a passion or sense that must absorb or hold in subjection the whole being; and he who is in possession of this sense of beauty must abhor vice and depravity of every kind. A beautiful face, glowing with the expression of a beautiful mind, leads us to seek for beauty in other objects; and in this way we attain to virtue, which is beauty partly earthly, partly divine, and from this we ascend to the sovereign beauty—the Creator of all things.

In the relations of the sexes, love must be limited to one object, and that for ever. Few lovers can observe this constancy, and few women can command it; for, in addition to charms of body, a woman must have a cultivated mind, grace, elegance, suavity of speech, good sense, and fidelity. Beauty and the eyes give birth to love; but if beauty fade, other graces remain which are not less dear to the heart. The senses open the door to love, but the soul must cherish a like sacred fire, and become purified by it. Such qualities must be directed by sensibility of heart, and appreciated by elevation and generosity of soul. When two persons meet under such conditions, she becomes more beautiful of soul, more wise, more happy in her affections; and he, to please her, must try to excel in virtue and beautify his soul, that he may emulate her moral and corporeal graces.

22. Such is an abstract of the theory of love as it was constructed by Lorenzo de Medici, and prefixed to his amatory poetry. I prefer to take it from such a source, since the writer knew under what inspiration the early Italian poets sang. There is abundant illustration of it to be found in Dante and other poets who preceded Petrarch, and it may be traced in the sonnets of Spenser and Shakspere, and in many poets of that later period.

But nowhere do we meet with so good a practical illustration of this theory as in the *Vita nuova* of Dante (19). It commences thus:—" In that part of the book of my memory (previous to which little can be read) a rubric occurs which says, *Incipit vita nova* (' Here begins a new life'); under which rubric I find written certain things which I intend to note down in this little book, at least in substance." He relates that, at the age of nine, " the glorious lady of his mind," namely, Beatrice, was seen by him for the first time. This was at Florence in 1274, at a May feast given by the father of Beatrice, Folco Portinari, to which Dante was taken by his father. She had just entered on her ninth year, and was clad in a crimson robe, girt and ornamented as befitted her age. "At this point I can truly say that the spirit of life, which dwells in the most secret chambers of the heart, began to tremble so strongly, that even the lesser pulses of my body partook of the commotion; and trembling it uttered these words

—*Ecce Deus fortior me, qui veniens dominabitur mihi* ('Behold a god stronger than I, who, coming, shall rule over me'). Whereupon the animate spirit that dwelleth in the high chamber [of the brain], to which all the sensitive spirits convey the perceptions, began greatly to marvel, and, speaking specially to the spirit of the eyes, uttered these words—*Apparuit jam beatitudo vestra* ('Your beatitude hath now appeared to you'). Whereupon the natural spirit that dwells in that part which ministers to our nourishment [that is, the vocal spirit] exclaimed, weeping, *Heu miser! quia frequenter impedibus ero deimceps* ('Woe is me! for from henceforth I shall often be disturbed'). I say that from that time love ruled my mind so completely, and with such sovereign rule, that by virtue of my strong imagination I was compelled to do his pleasure continually. He often commanded me to try and find out this youngest of the angels; and in my boyhood I often sought for her, and found her so noble and praiseworthy, that I could say of her in the words of Homer—'She seemed to be not the daughter of a mortal man, but of a god.'"

After a brief account of the progress of his love during some years, and how it inspired him to write verses, he describes the effect her salutation had on him.

"I say that when she appeared in any place the hope of her adorable salutation worked upon me in such a way that I seemed no longer to have an enemy, and such a glow of charity came over me that I could have forgiven any one who had offended me; and if any one had asked anything of me, my only reply would have been 'Love!' with humility depicted on my face. . . . . And when this most gentle lady saluted, love so far from being the means of overshadowing my intolerable beatitude, it produced in me such sovereign sweetness that my body, being wholly subject thereto, often became as it were an inanimate mass. Hence it was manifest that my beatitude was in her salutation, although it produced effects on me beyond my powers of endurance."

"This most gentle lady rose so much in favour with all men, that as she went along people ran to look at her; which rejoiced me greatly. And when she was near any one, so much truth entered his heart, that he dared not raise his eyes on her or return her salutation, as many can testify from experience. She went on her way crowned and clothed with humility, and displayed no pride at what she saw and heard. And when she had passed by, many said, 'That is not a woman, but one of the most beautiful angels of heaven!' And others said, 'This is a marvel! Blessed be the Lord who can work so admirably!' I say that she was so gentle and replete with every pleasant gift and grace, that those who looked on her experienced a sweet and tender feeling which cannot be described. And no one could look on her without sighing. These, and still more wonderful things, were produced by her marvellous virtue. Hence, thinking on these things, and wishing to devote something to her praise to embalm, as it were, her excellent and marvellous power, not only for the sake of those who had known her, but, so far as words could do it, to convey some idea of her to those who knew her not, to this end I wrote the following sonnet :—

$$\left.\begin{array}{l} 1\ 2\ 2\ 1,\ 1\ 2\ 2\ 1 \\ 3\ 4\ 5,\ 5\ 4\ 3. \end{array}\right\} \begin{array}{c} \textit{Tanto gentile e tanto} \\ \textit{onesta pare.} \end{array}$$

"When she, my lady, greets folk with 'Good-day,'
   Such candour and such gentleness combine,
   That tongues grow tremulous and speech resign,
And to look on her no one dare essay.
She feels men's praises as she goes her way
   In meekness clad, an influence benign;
   You fancy she must be a thing divine,
Come down from heaven, a marvel to display.
Her presence is so pleasant to the eye,
   That through the eye the heart with sweetness glows:
   To understand it, you its power must prove.
And from those lips an influence seems to move
   So sweet and full of love, it overflows,
   And goes on saying to our spirit, 'Sigh!'

"I have said that my lady grew so much in favour, that not only was she honoured and praised, but through her many others rose to honour and praise. Seeing this, and wishing to make it manifest to others who had not seen it, I wrote this sonnet, in which is expressed the power her virtue had on others of her own sex."[1]

23. When we consider the noble, impassioned nature of Petrarch, his poetical temperament, his strong devotional feeling and exquisite sense of beauty, and at the same time imbued as he was with the Platonic theory of love, the lofty language applied by him to Laura is accounted for. Not that his love was always Platonic, although he himself strove to make it so. There was an insuperable barrier between him and Laura, and whenever he approached her with more than usual fervour, her quiet self-possession was sufficient to repel him. That he loved her as he could love no other woman is certain; that, read by the eyes of his love, she possessed celestial beauty, is equally clear; but whether she ever sympathised with him during his long passion, is a secret that was never told. Certain it is, that Laura died without the suspicion of a stain on her character, and the sincerity of Petrarch's grief is proved by the more exalted style of his poetry in the *Morte* as compared with that in the *Vita*, beautiful and touching as this is. On hearing of her death Petrarch wrote in his favourite Virgil a note, of which the following is a portion:—" It was in the early days of my youth,

---

[1] The sonnet here referred to is given under (19.)

on the 6th of April, in the morning, and in the year 1327, that Laura, distinguished by her own virtues, and celebrated in my verses, first blessed my eyes in the church of Santa Clara, at Avignon; and it was in the same city, on the 6th of the very same month of April, at the very same hour in the morning, in the year 1348, that this bright luminary was withdrawn from our sight, when I was at Verona, alas! ignorant of my calamity. The remains of her chaste and beautiful body were deposited in the church of the Cordeliers on the evening of the same day."

In the expression of the sense of bereavement, Petrarch is all but unrivalled, and, like every one under such a condition, he inspires all nature in his verses with his own affliction. An example of this is to be found in the following plaintive sonnet. Some of loftier expression will be given in the course of these pages.

SONNET CCCXVII. } *Vago augelletto, che can-*
    TYPE II.   }   *tando vai.*

O wandering bird! that singest on thy way,
  Or mournest o'er the happy time gone by,
  Seeing the long, long nights and winter nigh,
  Bright days departed and the months so gay.
If, as thou know'st the cause of thy dismay,
  Thou knew'st the like sad state in which I sigh,
  Straight to this troubled bosom thou would'st fly,
  And blend with mine thy melancholy lay.

But yet I know not if thy lot be mine,
  For she may live for whom thou pour'st that strain :
  'Gainst me, alas! both Death and Heaven combine.
But as the hours their hue from winter gain,
  And sweet and bitter years their memories join,
  So I, in tender notes, with thee complain.

24. At the time when Petrarch wrote, the art of printing with movable types had yet to be discovered. The mode of publication was for the author to read his production to his friends or in public; or, if short, to distribute copies among those most likely to appreciate the work; and from these other copies were made, some of which, in the case of lyrical poems, were likely to find their way to the minstrel or ballad-singer, whose vocation required frequent additions to his stock-in-trade. In this way Petrarch's sonnets were eagerly sought after, and were heard, if not read, far and wide. Even before Laura's death they were so celebrated that at a *fête* given to the Emperor Charles IV. at Avignon, at which Laura was present, that sovereign desired that she might be introduced to him, and he kissed her on the forehead as a mark of respect for having inspired so many noble verses.

One of the sonnets placed near the beginning of Petrarch's collection (No. VII.) affords an example amongst others of the great popularity of the poet while yet young in his career as a song-writer. A young lady of Sasso Ferrato became attached to the muses, and so rare a taste at that period excited the ridicule of her relatives and friends. She was told that a woman's business was sewing and spinning; that it was not for her to aspire to the poetic laurel, but she was to throw away her pen and keep to the needle and the spindle. In her distress she wrote to Petrarch, and as the epistle at that time often took the form of the sonnet, so Justine de Levis Perrot addressed a sonnet to our poet, in which, with delicate flattery, she reminds him that by a bold flight he, still young, had gained the summit of Parnassus, would he deign to tell her what course to take? She wished to live after her death, and the muses alone could confer immortality on her. "Shall I devote myself to the muses, or resume my feminine duties, in order to escape the censure of the vulgar, who will not allow women to write verses, or to aspire to the laurel or myrtle crown?" Petrarch replied to this sonnet by another, technically known as an "Answering Sonnet," in which the same rhymes were repeated in the same order as in the effusion of the fair Justine. The scorn and aversion which Petrarch felt towards the age in which he lived were <u>sincere,</u> and are not limited to this sonnet.

SONNET VII. ⎫
TYPE III. ⎭ *La gola, e 'l sonno, e l'oziose piume.*

  Intemperance, Ease, and Pleasure's beds of down
    So rule the world, that every virtue's dead;
    And Nature's course is so by Fashion led,
    That her wise teaching men now scarcely own;
  And every light benign of Heaven is gone,
    By which life's path, in honour, we may tread;
    So that men gaze in wonder when 'tis said
    There are who feed the stream of Helicon.
  Thus speak the crowd, all basely bent on gain,
    "Who now the laurel crown or myrtle prize?
    Philosophy both poor and naked goes."
  Who court the Muse have few to sympathise.
    But, gentle Friend, strive not the less to obtain,
    The wreath that such high work as thine bestows.

This sonnet must have quickly passed into the mouths of the people, for it is related that a doctor in medicine meeting in the street a poor and ill-clad doctor in philosophy, quoted, in passing, the line from the first tercet,—

    Povera e nuda vai Filosofia.
    "Philosophy both poor and naked goes."

To which the philosopher promptly replied,—

    Dice la turba al vil guadagno intesa.
    "Thus speak the crowd all basely set on gain."

  25. It is no wonder then that if Petrarch's songs were so popular, the demand for them should go on

increasing in a higher ratio than the supply. In his letters to his friends, Petrarch laments having devoted his talents to the amusement of ballad-singers and lovers; but that his verses were too widely spread to be recalled, that many of them were inaccurate, and that some bearing his name were forgeries on the part of professional singers. He therefore determined in his old age to make a collection of the whole, rejecting those that were not authentic or not worthy of his muse. The first sonnet[1] may be regarded as a preface to this revised collection, the original of which is in the Vatican Library at Rome. The rejected pieces generally form the *Giunta alle Rime*, or "addition to the poems," in most editions of this author.

26. The minstrels who went about singing or reciting the poems of Messer Francesco Petrarca, were welcome not only in the houses of the aristocracy, but also among the burghers, and that these pieces were sung is not only evident from the derivation of the words "sonnet" and "canzone" already referred to (10), but the poet was accustomed to add musical notes to the stanzas. In some of the manuscript pieces of Sachetti and other contemporaries of Petrarch still preserved at Florence, the sonnets are occasionally headed—*Intonatum per Francum, Scriptor dedit Sonum.* We know also that Petrarch sang his verses to the sound of his lute, which he

[1] This is given among the illustrations in Part II.

bequeathed in his will to a friend, and we are told that his voice was sweet and flexible, and of considerable compass; it is also said that such was the magic of his song that the gravest persons were accustomed to go away repeating or humming the words. No wonder then that Petrarch became the idol of the people. His name was pronounced with a sort of adoration, and when he travelled the burghers prepared their houses to receive him, and he preferred them to the palaces of the great. A goldsmith of Padua not only had the Italian works and numerous portraits of the poet, but esteemed it as the proudest honour of his life to have received the poet as his guest. As he approached a town, princes, magistrates, and citizens went out to meet him, and on one occasion a blind old man made a long journey on foot, in the hope of being permitted to touch the poet's head.

The sonnets, as well as the canzoni, must have been committed to memory by vast numbers of Italians, who, as they could not possess the written copies in their hands, retained the songs themselves in their heads. To one of his friends who applied for a copy of his Italian poems, Petrarch replied:— "With what grace could I deny you verses which are current in the streets, and are in the mouth of all the world, who prefer them to the more solid compositions that I have produced in my riper years?" While thus unconsciously writing "the songs of the people," he was also labouring at his Latin epic and Latin treatises, which few cared to read (and now no one reads), and even resented the popularity of these lighter productions, he became by slow degrees conscious that wherever he went " the whole city came out to meet him," for the sake of these very verses which were " current in the streets," because they spoke the language of truth and nature, and found an echo in every one's heart. That Petrarch himself at length yielded to the popular expression is evident from the fact, already noticed, that he produced a revised edition of his Italian poems, and his reason for doing so is feelingly given in the following sonnet :—

SONNET CCLII. } *S' io avessi pensato, che si care.*
TYPE III.

Had I but thought my sighs, expressed in rhyme,
    Had aught in them the world would hold so dear,
    I would have sung, when Love at first drew near,
    In happier numbers, accents more sublime.
She who inspired my verse, dead in her prime,
    And wont in every thought of mine to appear,
    Could make my rough dark numbers, sweet and clear;
    But now such aid belongs no more to time.
Certain it was to ease my anguished breast,
    I know not how, that to the Muse I came ;
    I wept, but wept not for the poet's prize,
Nor deemed my verses worthy of their fame ;
    Now when I fain would please, her spirit blest
    Invites me, mute and weary, to the skies.

27. The above details furnish reasons why the Italian sonnet does not bear transplanting into English, or, indeed, into French or German soil. There are no sonnets in any one of these three languages that are in the mouths of the people in the sense that the songs of Burns are; for while these are native productions, the sonnet is an import, not suited to the taste of the multitude. Moreover, we are more cold and impassive than the Italians, and our poetry is rather the result of culture than of native impulse. Our most popular poetry is the song or ballad, which is best appreciated when it re-echoes our national sympathies, our home life, our political liberty, our national glory, our love of humour, of fair play, our hatred of cant and of shams. The single verse of Burns—

" It is good to be merry and wise,
  It is good to be honest and true,
It is good to be off with the old love
  Before you are on with the new,"

may not be a specimen of high-class poetry, but it includes both wisdom and wit happily expressed, those very qualities that the uncultured, because hitherto untaught, multitude best appreciate. Whereas one of Petrarch's sonnets, recited or sung to an Italian multitude, would excite enthusiasm. The Italian poet, captured by banditti, who saved himself and his party from spoliation by reciting his verses, would have no chance with English highwaymen, any more than our best English poet under similar conditions. The gondolier of Venice, who, singing a stanza of Tasso, was responded to by brother gondoliers in succeeding stanzas, has no equivalent among English boatmen.[1] But if one of the latter were to open out with—" And did you not hear of a jolly young waterman?" he would be not only keenly appreciated, but responded to by all his mates. I have heard French and Italian mechanics sing trios and quartets in harmony while engaged in their work. I have never heard English mechanics make such an attempt, although the Wilhem and the Tonic Sol-fa methods have been in operation during more than a quarter of a century. A single voice, however, engaged in singing "Black-eyed Susan," or "The Death of Nelson," or "The Bay of Biscay, O," would not fail to excite their enthusiasm.

28. The best English sonnets, according to the Italian type, are, in my opinion, those of Milton; and his Italian sonnets are ranked by Italian critics on a level with those of Parini, which is high praise. Although Milton does not always close his second

---

[1] Goldoni, in his autobiography, thus refers to the gondolier who took him back to Venice :—" He turned the prow of his gondola towards the city, singing all the way the twenty-sixth stanza of the sixteenth canto of the Gerusalemme." A lady, now resident in Venice, informs me that some of the gondoliers can recite Tasso, although they cease to sing his verses. She heard a picturesque mendicant recite Tasso in the street. An account of the practice, when in full vogue among the gondoliers, is given in D'Israeli's *Curiosities of Literature*, i. p. 389.

quatrain with a full point, and is not sufficiently varied in his rhymes, he is closer to the Italian type than any other English poet. After what has been said, the following arrangement of Milton's sonnets may be interesting:—

$$\text{TYPE I.} \begin{cases} 1\ 2\ 2\ 1,\ 1\ 2\ 2\ 1, \\ 3\ 4\ 5,\ 3\ 4\ 5. \end{cases}$$

No. 9. Daughter to that good Earl, once President
12. Lady, that in the prime of earliest youth
17. Vane, young in years, but in sage counsel old
19. When I consider how my light is spent
21. Cyriac, whose grandsire, on the royal bench.

$$\text{TYPE II.} \begin{cases} 1\ 2\ 2\ 1,\ 1\ 2\ 2\ 1, \\ 3\ 4\ 3,\ 4\ 3\ 4. \end{cases}$$

No. 1. O Nightingale! that on yon bloomy spray
8. Captain, or colonel, or knight in arms
10. A book was writ of late call'd Tetrachordon
14. When Faith and Love, which parted from thee never
18. Avenge, O Lord! thy slaughter'd saints, whose bones
22. Cyriac, this three years day these eyes, though clear
23. Methought I saw my late espoused saint.

$$\text{TYPE III.} \begin{cases} 1\ 2\ 2\ 1,\ 1\ 2\ 2\ 1, \\ 3\ 4\ 5,\ 4\ 3\ 5. \end{cases}$$

No. 2. *Donna leggiadra, il cui bel nome honora*
6. *Giovane piano, e semplicette amante*
7. How soon hath Time, the subtle thief of youth
13. Harry, whose tuneful and well-measured song.

Hence it appears that in sixteen out of the twenty-three sonnets, or more than two-thirds, the metrical arrangement follows the most approved Italian types; and among these sixteen examples are to be found nearly all Milton's very best sonnets. In the remaining seven the quatrains are still the same as in the sixteen examples given. The variations are in the tercets. For example, under

3 4 4, 3 4 3

we have—

No. 11. I did but prompt the age to quit their clogs
    15. Fairfax, whose name in arms through Europe rings.

Under 3 4 3, 4 5 5

No. 3. *Qual in colle aspro, al imbrunir di sera*
    4. *Diodati, e te 'l dirò con maraviglia,*
    5. *Per certo i bei vostr 'occhi, Donna mia*
   16. Cromwell, our chief of men, who through a cloud;

and under 3 4 3, 5 5 4,

No. 20. Lawrence, of virtuous father virtuous son.

29. On attempting to make a similar analysis of the first thirty of Wordsworth's Duddon sonnets, it was found impossible to do so. Although the poet evidently endeavoured to keep the quatrains tolerably regular, he could not, or did not, prevent the tercets from running wildly; so that there are no less than twenty-two variations in these thirty

sonnets; while in Milton's there are but three—
that is, three regular types and three variations.
Moreover, there is no clear distinction between the
quatrains and the tercets, which often run into each
other; and the tercets are frequently used, not for
the sake of drawing a conclusion from the matter
laid down in the quatrains, but merely for carrying
on the description of some spot, or feature of a spot,
with which the sonnet opened. Hence these sonnets
do not in many cases bear to be dissociated from
their fellows, because it may happen that if one be
taken out and presented as a specimen of an Eng-
lish sonnet, it would be unintelligible for want of
the context. Hence I cannot help thinking it was
unfortunate that Wordsworth should have selected
this form for a continuous narrative or connected
series. A sonnet ought to be a complete organic
structure, capable of being separated and admired
for itself, without reference to its position in a
collection. That the sonnets of Petrarch and of the
other great Italian masters stand this test, is due to
the fact that their authors endeavoured to conform
rigidly to the exactions of the little poem (12); to
write, in fact, according to rule as regarded the form
and purpose, whatever might be the thought to be
elaborated. Whereas in many of Wordsworth's
sonnets there is a looseness in structure and treat-
ment that is opposed to the theory of this produc-
tion. Take almost any one of them, and it will

not be found to contain a proposition, a proof, and a conclusion, but a meditation, or a thought, or more often a description exquisitely expressed in fourteen lines; but the reader does not feel the necessity for this limitation, and may ask why it should be in fourteen lines?—why not in twenty, or, in some cases, still better, in ten? It would be difficult to answer these questions, except by remarking that many of Wordsworth's so-called sonnets are not sonnets at all, according to the Italian definition; but it must also be added, that whenever he submits to that definition, whether consciously or not, and has some respect for the harmony of the form, the thought becomes more sharply defined and elaborated, and the result is not only Wordsworth's best sonnet, but an English sonnet deserving of the name. If I were called upon to justify this statement by an example, I should be disposed to cite the sonnet to Haydon. It is regularly built up according to the first type—the second quatrain terminates in a full point, and the tercets in alternate rhyme lead happily to a noble conclusion. The sonnet of Wordsworth, which is perhaps the most admired among upwards of three hundred that he wrote, commencing

"Surprised by joy—impatient as the wind,"

has a strong Petrarchan flavour. Although loose in structure, it reads like a good, but free, translation of one of the early sonnets in the *Morte*.

30. Although Milton's sonnets approach nearest to the Italian form, they made but little impression on the course of English literature; for in the long interval between Milton and Cowper, occupied as it is by such great names as Cowley, Waller, Marvel, Dryden, Pope, Gay, Parnell, Collins, Shenstone, Akenside, Young, Thomson, Johnson, Goldsmith, Churchill, and others, the sonnet was neglected. Gray revived it, if a single specimen can be said to be a revival. His sonnet, or rather pleasant little poem in fourteen lines, begins thus—

"In vain to me the smiling mornings shine."

Mason's sonnet, commencing

"A plaintive sonnet flowed from Milton's pen,"

is regular, and after the Italian model; as is also Warton's,

"Oh! what a weary race my feet have run,"

and Roscoe's,

"As one who destined from his friends to part."

But all these must rather be regarded as scholarly exercises than spontaneous bursts of thought, which mark the true sonnet, and did nothing to naturalise the little poem.

Bowles is regarded as the reviver of the sonnet in recent literature; but his efforts in this way, though sweet and pensive, are loose in structure, and show no reason why they should each be limited to fourteen lines.

31. Referring to the time anterior to that of Milton, the word sonnet immediately recalls the splendid names of Spenser and Shakspere, whose productions I do not venture to criticise, except to remark that they do not follow the Italian model, but consist of three elegiac stanzas of four lines each, in alternate rhyme, and finishing with a rhymed couplet. But there is this difference in the form adopted, namely, that while Spenser connects his second stanza with the first, and the third with the second, by taking up the closing rhyme of each stanza for the first and third lines of the next; Shakspere does not fetter his pen with any such arrangement. The two forms may be thus represented graphically :—

Spenser.	*Shakspere.*
1 2 1 2,	1 2 1 2,
2 3 2 3,	3 4 3 4,
3 4 3 4,	5 6 5 6,
5 5.	7 7.

The writers of this time had no concurrent agreement to introduce the Italian sonnet to the English muse, although some of them came near to it. Sir Walter Raleigh, in his Vision upon the Faery Queen,

"Methought I saw the grave where Laura lay,"

adopts Shakspere's arrangement; as does also, with

some variations, the Earl of Surrey, who is regarded as the father of the English sonnet. One of his most celebrated sonnets usually given in our anthologies, and lately by Trench (*Household Book of English Poetry*), as a specimen of the noble poet's style, and also placed first in the list of *English* sonnets in Mr. Dennis's collection (1873), is really a pretty close translation of Petrarch's 113th sonnet, commencing *Ponmi, ove 'l Sol,* etc., and the idea running through this is an elaboration of the passage in the 22d ode of Horace—

Pone me pigris ubi nulla campis, etc.

I give (i.) the original Italian, (ii.) my English version, and (iii.) Surrey's translation, in which it will be seen that no attempt is made to follow the metrical arrangement of the Italian poet.

Sonnet CXIII. Type II.

Ponmi, ove 'l Sol occide i fiori e l' erba ;[1]
O dove vince lui 'l ghiaccio e la neve :
Ponmi ov' è 'l carro suo temprato e leve ;
Ed ov' è chi cel rende, o chi cel serba :
Ponm' in umil fortuna, od in superba ;
Al dolce aere sereno, al fosco e greve :

---

[1] This Sonnet was made the subject of three lectures by Bonsi before the *Accademia della Crusca*, on the 6th, 13th, and 20th November 1550. They contain a large amount of curious detail respecting the geography and astronomy (then called astrology) of the time.

Ponmi alla notte, al di lungo, ed al breve;
Alla matura etate, od all acerba:
Ponm' in cielo, od in terra, od in abisso;
In alto poggio, in valle ima e palustre;
Libero spirto, od a' suoi membri affisso:
Ponmi con fama oscura, o con illustre:
Sarò qual fui; vivrò com' io son visso,
Continuando il mio sospir trilustre.

(ii.) Place me where Sol burns up the grass and flower,
  Or where the ice and snow o'ercome his rays;
  Place me where rolls his car with temperate blaze,
  In climes that know not, or that own his power.
Place me where Fortune smiles, or seems to lour:
  'Neath murky sky, or where the zephyr plays;
  Place me in night, in long or shorter days,
  In age mature, or in youth's careless hour.
Place me in heaven, on earth, in deepest sea,
  On mountain high; in marshy valley lone;
  Whether I live, or Death possesses me;
Place me where Fame may own me or disown:
  I still live on, as I was wont to be,
  Still breathing out the same trilustral moan.

(iii.) SURREY'S TRANSLATION.

Set me whereas the sun doth parch the green,
Or where his beams do not dissolve the ice;
In temperate heat, where he is felt and seen;
In presence prest of people mad or wise;
Set me in high, or yet in low degree;
In longest night, or in the shortest day;
In clearest sky, or where clouds thickest be;
In lusty youth, or when my hairs are grey:

> Set me in heaven, in earth, or else in hell,
> In hill or dale, or in the foaming flood;
> Thrall, or at large, alive whereso I dwell,
> Sick or in health, in evil fame or good,
> Hers will I be; and only with this thought
> Content myself, although my chance be nought.

Mr. Dennis, in a note (p. 201), gives a version of a sonnet published in London in 1593 by an anonymous writer, which he says "bears a curious resemblance to Surrey's sonnet." This is only one more of the many forms of translation of Petrarch's sonnet. It is, therefore, with some little amusement that I read the remark of Warton, also quoted by Mr. Dennis (p. 199), that "in the sonnets of Surrey we are surprised to find nothing of that metaphysical cast which marks the Italian poets, his supposed masters, especially Petrarch. Surrey's sentiments are, for the most part, natural and unaffected; arising from his own feelings, and dictated by the present circumstances."

Drummond was also supersaturated with Petrarch, and although a good poet on his own account, could not help adopting the mode and sometimes the language of his model. The very title of his book, "Sonnets, Songs, Sextains, Madrigals," calls to mind Petrarch with his "*Sonetti, Canzoni, Ballate, Sestine, e Madrigale.*" In his clear, sweet, and soft expression, he justifies the epithet of "the Scottish Petrarch" bestowed upon him. His sonnets

"Vaunt not fair heaven of your too glorious lights;"

and

"Sweet soul, which in the April of thy years
' Go to enrich the heaven, mad'st poor this round,"

are thoroughly Petrarchan; and in some cases his sonnets are free renderings from the Italian. For example, the first quatrain of Petrarch's 233d sonnet runs as follows:—

> *Datemi pace, o duri miei pensieri :*
> *Non basta ben, ch' Amor, Fortuna e Morte*
> *Mi fanno guerra intorno, e 'n su le porte,*
> *Senza trovarmi dentro altri guerrieri ?*

Drummond's—

> Ah, burning thoughts! now let me take some rest,
> And your tumultuous broils awhile appease;
> Is't not enough, stars, fortune, love molest
> Me all at once, but ye must too displease?

My translation—

> Hard thoughts of mine, oh, give me some repose!
> Is't not enough that Love, and Death, and Fate,
> Make war around, up to my very gate,
> But I must find within me other foes?

32. It must, however, be considered that about the period when Drummond wrote, the comparatively small number of readers who could appreciate him were also admirers of Petrarch, and any

adaptations from the Italian masters rather justified the scholarship of the later poet than suggested anything like what we call plagiarism. Thus we see Chaucer transferring to his Troylus and Cryseyde, a sonnet of Petrarch, the 102d, commencing

> *S'amor non è; che dunque è quel ch' i' sento ?*

which in Chaucer's hands becomes:—

> "If no love is, O God, what fele I so ?" v. 58.[1]

Spenser also appropriates two whole stanzas of Tasso, namely, the beautiful description of the rose, beginning

> *Deh mira (egli cantò) spuntar la rosa*
> *Dal verde suo modesta, e verginella.*

Indeed, if we compare Spenser's Canto xii. of the "Faerie Queene," with Tasso's Canto xvi. of the *Gerusalemme*, we shall find how largely Spenser borrowed from Tasso. If we examine Tasso with earlier writers, it will be seen that he is constantly borrowing whenever it suits his purpose to do so. Thus in the charming opening of the *Gerusalemme*, he apologises for mixing truth and fiction, on the ground that when physic is given to a sick child it is customary to smear the edge of the cup with a

---

[1] Leigh Hunt seems to have supposed that Chaucer was ignorant of the Italian sonnet. He says:—" Had Chaucer been familiar with the sonnets of men whom he so admired, the very lovingness of his nature would hardly have failed to make him echo their tones."—*Book of the Sonnet*, i. 65.

sweet. This idea is from Lucretius "Sed veluti pueris, etc." The well-known *materiam superabat opus* of Ovid is taken advantage of in describing the hilt of Argantes's sword (Canto ii., v. 93); while passages, to be counted by dozens, from Virgil and others are simply translated, or adapted, according to the wants of the poet. All this is done quite openly, and although there are no marginal references, there is not the slightest suspicion of wrongdoing. The classics were so well known, that the reader of Tasso, or other modern poet, would be glad to recognise old friends among the many new ones the Italian poet introduced to his notice. Of course this sort of thing could only be done with impunity by men of such exalted intellectual rank as Tasso, Ariosto, Spenser, etc. They had lavished so much native wealth on their poems, that, while justifying their own scholarship, it seemed rather in the way of a compliment to older authors to use them occasionally, than to supply their own deficiencies by this practice; and this was so well known, that it continued down to what date I cannot say. Certain it is, that in the time of Milton the practice had assumed another form; for although the Paradise Lost, as was first pointed out by Addison, contains much material derived from the ancients, it is as material only, to be transmuted in the working, that the ancient writers are laid under tribute. In the time of Pope the practice had again changed, and admitted "Imitations of Horace" are made the vehicle of much original thought, wittily and happily expressed. The practice of borrowing ideas without acknowledgment had become so censurable in the time of Voltaire as to justify the sarcasm of Piron, who, being present at the reading of one of Voltaire's plays, was observed frequently to bow. On being asked why he did so, he replied "Never mind me! it is only a habit I have of recognising an old acquaintance." If the history of plagiarism ever comes to be written, it will present as varied a picture as any other phase of human thought. The historian will have to trace the steps by which a laudable and admitted practice became censurable and forbidden. I suppose the practice wore itself out, and readers of taste became tired of seeing classical mixed up with modern thought, especially on the part of many who were not Spensers or Tassos. Most readers will remember how severely censured were the poems of Alexander Smith, which were supposed to contain other men's thoughts wrapped up in his own language; and I confess to a kind of shudder when a great poet like Byron appropriates a master thought as in his Nature "broke the die in moulding Sheridan," which is but a translation of Ariosto's famous

Natura lo fece e poi ruppe la stampa.

Many other similar examples might be cited, and

they are tolerated only in the case of intellectual capitalists, who may be excused if, among their own countless gold pieces, another man's stray coin should sometimes be found.

33. Petrarch, in his Italian verses, borrows very sparingly from the Latin classical writers, with whom he was well acquainted; and his abstinence is on principle. His respect for the Latin poets was so deep, that it seemed a kind of sacrilege to adapt them to the *rime volgare*. Nevertheless, Ugo Foscolo is wrong in supposing that only two or three passages in Petrarch can be traced back to a classical source. There are more than two or three, but still not a large number. A few examples may be given, the first of which is from Virgil—

Agnovit longe gemitum præsaga mali mens

which seems to have suggested

Mente mia che presaga de 'tuoi danni
My mind, prophetic of my coming loss.

And Ovid's

Elige cui dicas, tu mihi sola places.
A cui io dissi—Tu sola a me piace.
To whom I said—"Thou only pleasest me."

Horace's

Dulce ridentem Lalagen amabo
Dulce loquentem

is more poetical and tender in Petrarch's

> *Che non sa come dolce ella sospira,*
> *E come dolce parla e dolce ride.*

Who knows not how she sweetly sighs,
And how she sweetly speaks, and sweetly smiles.

So also the verse of Horace

> Et tinctus viola pallor amantium

is thus rendered

> *Un pallor di viola, e d'amor tinto*

" As fear or shame my pallid cheek arrayed
In violet hues, with Love's thick blushes strown."
Wrangham.

Petrarch frequently derives his illustrations from Holy Scripture, showing that at the time its books were scattered and not easy of access, he was well acquainted with them, as befitted his pious nature. One or two examples may suffice—

" My harp also is turned to mourning."—Job xxx. 31.

> *E la cetera mia rivolta è in pianto.*—Son. CCLI.

" The spirit indeed is willing but the flesh is weak." Matt. xxvi. v. 41.

> *Lo spirto e pronta, ma la carne è stanca.*—Son. CLXXIII.

In the following sonnet are two illustrations from Matthew xi. 28, and Psalm lv. 6.

SONNET LX. } *Io son si stanco sotto 'l fascio*
TYPE III. }   *antico.*

I feel all weary 'neath the accustomed weight
    Of my old sins, and habits formed of sin;
    And fear, lest fainting on the road I'm in,
    I fall a victim to the power I hate.
Time was, a mighty friend compassionate,
    To rescue me came of His grace benign,
    And then departed; and I cannot win
    Another look, although I longing, wait.
But yet I hear his words, all steeped in love;
"All ye that labour, see! the road is here,
    That leads to me, then heed no other quest."
What grace, or love, or fate will grant this prayer:—
"And oh, that I had pinions like a dove!
    For then I'd fly away and be at rest."

Sonnet CCXCVIII. commences thus—

    The food which fed my Lord did never fail;
        Sorrows and tears feed too my weary heart:
        I always tremble, and my cheek grows pale,
        Thinking of his deep wounds and bitter smart.

In one of my copies of Petrarch, edited by Zotti (London, 1811), the editor has a note on the word "my Lord." Evidently supposing that the poet could only write about love, he explains the term *'l Signor mio* as *il mio Signor Amore.*

34. The charge has often been brought against Petrarch, and was made even in his own time, that

he is indebted to the troubadours and Provençals for much of his poetry. There is evidence in the works of all the poets, from Dante to Petrarch, of an intimate knowledge of this older poetry; but it is too much to say that in selected passages containing similar thoughts the later poet must have borrowed from the earlier. The language of poetry, like the song of birds, is natural; and under like conditions produces like results. But, in addition to this common expression, a great poet has an original language of his own, by which he lives and is recognised. And herein he is distinguished from the man of science, whose works reflect not his own individuality, but simply nature. The language in which he makes known his discoveries is of less importance than the discoveries themselves; they become absorbed into the great body of science, and the man and his style are to a great extent forgotten, just as an individual link in a chain is forgotten in the chain itself. But it is not so in literature, least of all in poetry. The poet may make as many discoveries as the chemist, or the physicist, or the astronomer: he may read nature as accurately, and may work as beneficently, but he cannot be separated from his work: he has impressed upon it the individual characters of his own mind, so that a page of Dante or of Shakspere, however true for all time, is still the truth, tinged by Dante's or Shakspere's individuality; whereas a page of Newton or of Faraday is valuable only as it reflects nature and nature only.

The reason why the poetry of the troubadour and of the Provençals has only an antiquarian interest is, that although it contains much that is elegant and natural, it is monotonous and affected, the poems of one author having a strong family likeness to those of another, so that, like the lace and ruffles and powdered head-dresses of a later period, they reflect not human nature, but rather a transient fashion; a mode of writing which, however useful as a means to something better, could not be permanent, because it was not distinguished by grand, original, and striking thoughts, which appeal to us as much by their inherent truth as by the style and manner in which they are put forth. We therefore prove nothing if it can be shown that Dante and Petrarch uttered a thought that had already occurred to an older poet; or we only prove that simple thoughts, which naturally spring up with the occasion that calls them forth, are common property. For example, Petrarch expresses the very old idea that against love neither force nor skill are of any avail—

Contro lo qual non val forza ne ingegno,

and he is accused of having taken this very commonplace idea from Bonello—

Mas vas amors no val forsa nè torre
('Gainst love nor force nor battlement avails.)

Petrarch more than once declares that he had resolved to say many fine things to Laura, but as soon as he found himself in her presence, a glance from her bright eyes made him silent. What more natural than this? The troubadour Pier delle Vigne has a similar thought—

Ma, poi la veo, oblio ciò ch' ho pensato
(But when I see her, I forget what I thought of.)

Both these have been claimed for Arnaud Daniell.

C'ades ses lieis die a lieis cochez mots—
Fois, quan la vei, no sai, tan l'am, que dire.

(Without her—*i.e.*, far from her—I say to her loving words; but when I see her, so much I love her, I know not what to say.)

Once more, was there ever a swain in love who did not swear to his lady that he would rather die for her than live in bliss with another.

E plaz mi mais morir per vos,
Que per antra viver ioios.

Petrarch says the same thing more elegantly—

Pur mi consola che languir per lei,
Meglio è che gioir d'altra.

Until it can be shown that the noble and beautiful thoughts which crowd the pages of Dante and Petrarch, and the surpassing style of each, are borrowed, such small charges as those referred to have no effect on their fame, even when they are as gravely brought forward as in the case of the historian of Valentia, Gasparo Scuolano, who says—"We formerly possessed a famous poet, named Mossen Jordi; and Petrarch, who was born a hundred years after, robbed him of his verses, and has sold them in Italian to the world as his own, of which I could convict him in many passages; however, I shall content myself with quoting a few lines:—

> ' E non he pau, e no tin quim guerreig;
> Vol sobre l'ciel, et nom' movi de terra;
> E no estrench res, e tot lo mon abras,
> Oy he de mi, e vull a altri gran be—
> Si no es amor, donchs azo' que sera?' "

The following is Petrarch's sonnet, based upon this rough fragment:—

SONNET CIV.
First Variation
of the Quatrains.
} *Pace non trovo, e non ho da far guerra.*

I find not peace; for war too weak am I;
  I fear and hope and burn; like ice am cold;
  I soar beyond heaven's gate; on earth I lie;
  Nothing I have, yet all the world enfold.
My jailer doth not bind, nor yet untie;
  Doth not release me, nor in prison hold:

Love slays me not, nor loosens his firm tie;
  Doth not give life, nor care from me withhold.
Having no eyes, I see; no tongue, complain;
  I wish to perish, and yet cry for aid;
  I love another, yet myself I hate;
I feed myself on grief; I laugh in pain,
  And death and life alike are hateful made:
  For thee, O lady, I am in this state.

Mr. Rutherford (*The Troubadours: their Lives and their Lyrics*, 1873) says "that Dante, Petrarch, Ariosto, and Tasso, to make no mention of lesser names, paraphrased as extensively from the Provençals as Spenser of the Faerie Queene and some other early English bards paraphrased from the Italians. . . . If the appropriation of a man's ideas be conferring honour on him, then we must say that Petrarch distributed a good deal of honour among the troubadours," p. 349. In justification of this sweeping charge, Mr. Rutherford gives one line of Petrarch from the 47th sonnet—

Benedetto sia 'l giorno, e 'l mese, e 'l anno,

and refers to a parallel line in a canzon attributed to Giraud of Borneil—

Ben ai al temps, et jorn, e 'l an, e 'l mes.
(Blessed be the season, the day, the year, the month.)

"The plagiarism," he says, "is curious, and not the less so, since precisely the same benediction is repeated by Byron:—

> "Ave Marie! Blessed be the hour!
> The time, the clime, the spot!"

Is this "precisely the same benediction?" Such charges as these, however, are not uncommon; and they may be met by the fact that a great writer may, and does often, borrow the lead of small men, and by a rare alchemy transmutes it into gold. Shakspere was in the habit of doing this, and those are among the dullest books that attempt to justify the proof. If the reader is curious to see a specimen of this kind, he had better compare Dr. Ferriar's *Illustrations of Sterne* with *Tristram Shandy*.

Petrarch was too near the time of the troubadours not to be influenced by them. That he occasionally imitated their manner, and improved upon their matter, may be admitted; and as an example of the manner, the following sonnet may be quoted. It is, as Sismondi remarks, a mosaic of antitheses, and, as such, worthy of the school it belongs to:—

SONNET CLXXXVIII. *S'una fede amorosa,*
TYPE I.   *un cor non finto.*

> If loving faith, a heart that does not feign,
>   Sweet languor and a courteous desire;
>   If honest wishes burn with gentle fire;
>   If wand'ring long a labyrinth in vain;
> If in the face each thought is written plain,
>   Or faltering accents on the lips expire;

> If bashfulness or fear should kindle ire;
> If pallid cheek, lit by love's blushing stain;
> If more than self, to hold another dear;
> If sighs for aye, if tears ne'er cease to flow,
> Feeding on anger and in grief to pine,
> Burning in absence, all too chilled when near;
> If these be causes why love brings me woe,
> Thine lady is the crime, the suffering mine.

35. I have now to consider the duties imposed on the translator in dealing with the masterpieces of the great Italian sonnet-writers. His first duty is to define clearly to himself upon what principles he intends to work, seeing that the laws which ought to guide a translator, in dealing with his original, are by no means settled. On the one hand, it is contended that the translation should have the effect on the reader's mind of an original work; and, on the other, that the effect should be that of an imitation, or a copy of the original in an inferior material, but resembling it as closely as such material will allow. This method has been named *metaphrase*, or literal rendering, and the former *paraphrase*, or loose rendering. Dryden in his translation of Virgil professes to have steered a middle course between the two methods; but he adds, " Some things I have omitted, and sometimes have added of my own. Yet the omissions I hope are but of circumstances, and such as would have no grace in English; and the additions I also hope

are easily deduced from Virgil's sense. They will seem (at least I have the vanity to think so) not stuck into, but growing out of him."

This is a perilous example for a young translator to follow, and the instance that Dryden gives to justify his practice seems to me rather to condemn it. In the first Æneid, Venus places Cupid on a bed of *Mollis Amaracus*. " If," continues Dryden, " I should translate it 'Sweet Marjoram,' as the word signifies, the reader would think I had mistaken Virgil. For these village words, as I may call them, give us a mean idea of the thing; but the sound of the Latin is so much more pleasing by the just mixture of the vowels with the consonants, that it raises our fancies to conceive somewhat more noble than a common herb; and to spread roses under him and strew lilies over him; a bed not unworthy the grandson of the goddess."

In practice Dryden does not adopt the roses and lilies, but employs a more general expression :—

" Then with a wreath of myrtle crowns his head,
 And softly lays him on a flowery bed."

But a man of Dryden's power is not to be lightly dismissed. On examining his statements a little more closely, it must be admitted that they contain a true principle. Undoubtedly there are words and modes of thought which have a poetical effect in one language and not in another; and it is the translator's duty to substitute other words and modes of thought, taking care, in doing so, to make them grow out of the original, and not stick them into it. To do this properly requires sound judgment and correct taste. Many illustrations of this occur in Petrarch. For example, in that vigorous sonnet in which the poet denounces the vices of the Papal Court at Avignon, the first tercet runs as follows:—

> *Per le camere tue fanciulle e vecchi*
> *Vanno trescando, e Belzebub in mezzo*
> *Co' mantici, e col foco, e con gli specchi.*

"Through thy chambers young girls and old men go dancing, Beelzebub in the midst, with bellows, fire, and mirrors." The mirrors seem to be typical of vanity, and the bellows the incentives which fan the unholy fire (*foco*) on the hearth of sin; but he would be a bold man who ventured to translate this literally, even supposing a literal translation capable of being understood; whereas the original may be perfectly intelligible to the Italian mind. I do not say that it is, because Muratori, being a priest, probably thought it judicious to offer no comments on this sonnet, and the only commentator, so far as I know, who has a note on the third line of the tercet, is Zotti, who interprets *coi mantici* by the somewhat vague expression "with amorous incentives," and merely adds to *col foco* the words *d'amore.* I have endeavoured to meet the difficulty by the following compromise:—

> Old men and damsels through thy chambers glide,
>   Ringing the changes of sin's varied mood,
>   In wanton glee, Beelzebub their guide.

But I do not pretend to say that this is satisfactory. It is a far more difficult case than that of Venus with her bed of sweet marjoram, which, however, does not strike me as unpoetical; and, with all deference to so great a master as Dryden, I should have given it in my translation instead of the more vague expression which he adopts, or the roses and lilies which he would have preferred.

36. The sonnets of Petrarch require a very tender handling on the part of the translator; and this they have not always received from the numerous hands that have attempted to render them into English verse. The introduction of high-sounding words, or the translator's ideas instead of those of the author, is all but certain to injure the original; and the injury becomes more painfully prominent when the translator, as is sometimes the case, approaches his subject with an imperfect knowledge of the Italian language. So also any attempt to change the order of the lines generally interrupts the sequence of the thought and is injurious. Moreover, it is nearly always necessary to render the original line for line, although this cannot

always be done, since some lines are too full for the English, and others not full enough (12). Nevertheless, it may be taken as a general rule, that a line-for-line translation gives the most satisfactory result, because it more nearly represents the original.

As nothing better illustrates a general proposition than an example, I venture to take one out of a large number that may be selected, and that one is from the tercets of the 126th Sonnet. The following is the original:—

> *Per divina bellezza indarno mira,*
> *Chi gli occhi di costei giammai non vide,*
> *Come soavemente ella gli gira.*
> *Non sa com 'Amor sana, e come ancide,*
> *Chi non sa come dolce ella sospira,*
> *E come dolce parla, e dolce ride.*

In this example, the weakest poetical sense must feel the exquisite simplicity of the expression, and that any departure from it can only mar its beauty. In attempting a translation, it is evident that the closing line *must* be rendered literally—

"And how she sweetly speaks and sweetly smiles."

Nothing else will do. The line before it also requires similar treatment. But there is this difficulty; the line—

"Who knows not how she sweetly sighs,"

is not long enough, and the introduction of any

other word not in the original would disturb the simplicity of a picture that is already finished and complete. The least objectionable course seemed to lie in the repetition of the word "sweetly;" so that the line runs thus :—

"Who knows not how she sweetly, sweetly sighs."

But the literal rendering of these two lines, whether satisfactory or not, introduces another difficulty. The sonnet belongs to Type II., in which the six lines of the tercets run in alternate rhymes; and two more rhymes are wanted for "sighs" and two for "smiles." "Eyes" in the first tercet gives one, and "beguiles" another, but I could not discover two others without straining the meaning, which is opposed to my canon. But as Dryden remarks that the necessity for a rhyme often suggests an idea, so in this case it suggested a resource. The word "gaze" in the first tercet suggested "slays" in the second, which is the accurate rendering of *ancide*, and hence the idea occurred to me to translate these tercets after the model of Type I., namely—3 4 5, 3 4 5, instead of that of Type II., 3 4 3, 4 3 4. I was sorry thus to infringe upon the rule laid down in these translations; but as fidelity to the sense is evidently of more importance than adherence to the form, this course was adopted, and the following result is, I trust, not unsatisfactory :—

> He vainly seeks on charms divine to gaze,
>   Who never gazed upon those lovely eyes,
>   How their sweet turning every soul beguiles:
> He knows not how Love heals, nor how Love slays,
>   Who knows not how she sweetly, sweetly sighs,
>   And how she sweetly speaks and sweetly smiles.

37. So also it may not unfrequently happen that in one of Petrarch's sonnets a single line stands out in such eminent beauty, that it is absolutely necessary to the integrity of the translation that this line at least be rendered literally, however difficult it may be to make the other verses conform to it. An example of this may be selected from Sonnet CCLI., in which the poet, after enumerating the charms of Laura, says—

> *Poca polvere son, che nulla sente.*
> Are now a little dust, that nothing feels.

The volume referred to below [1] gives four translations of this sonnet, in which the line in question is thus variously rendered:—

> " A little dust are now! to feeling cold."
> *Dacre.*

> " What are they now? Dust, lifeless dust, alas!"
> *Morehead.*

---

[1] In 1859 Mr. Bohn published a collection of translations, entitled "The Sonnets, Triumphs, and other Poems of Petrarch, now first completely translated into English verse, by various hands, with a Life of the Poet by Thomas Campbell."

> "Are now a pile of ashes, deadly cold."
> *Woodhouselee.*

> "Dissolved to senseless ashes now remain."
> *Charlemont.*

A body does not *dissolve* into ashes. But I think it must be admitted that all these variations are inferior to the original verse, which can be so easily translated literally; and to show that there are no great difficulties in making the other verses conform to this one, I append my translation, the only merit of which I consider to lie in a greater closeness to the original than in the efforts of my predecessors. I may also remark that the last line of this sonnet requires literal treatment, not only because it is a quotation from Holy Scripture, but also because it best expresses the original:—

> *E la cetera mia rivolta in pianto.*
> My harp is turned to mourning.

Of the four translators of this sonnet already referred to, the first gives this line best, because nearest to the original:—

> "And turned to mourning my once tuneful lyre."

The second—

> "Mute be the lyre, tears best my sorrow mark."

The third omits the line altogether, and expands two lines of the original into three of his own.

The fourth—

"Changed is my lyre, attuned to endless woe."

SONNET CCLI. } *Gli occhi di ch' io parlai si*
TYPE II.   *caldamente.*

The eyes of which my verse so warmly tells,
    The face, arms, hands, and feet, that bright array
    Of charms that steal me from myself away,
    And every act of mine with strangeness fills:
The crispèd hair that lucent gold reveals,
    The angelic smile, that seemed a heavenly ray,
    Pointing from earth to paradise the way,
    Are now a little dust, that nothing feels.
And yet I live; but live in grief and pain,
    Deprived of her, my much-loved guiding light,
    In tempest fierce, with shattered bark amain.
But from my amorous muse I now take flight,
    Dried up my poesie's accustomed vein,
    My harp is turned to mourning and 'tis night.

The last line of this sonnet, *E la cetera mia rivolta in pianto*, translated into the language of Scripture, "My harp is turned to mourning," is not long enough. But on referring to Job, ch. xxx., from which the passage is taken (v. 31), these words occur at v. 28: "I went mourning without the sun;" and hence it seems to be taking not too great a liberty with the quotation, or with the sonnet, to make up the verse by the words, "and 'tis night."

It may, however, be a question whether the second line of the first quatrain—

E le braccia, e le mani, e i piedi, e 'l viso,

ought to be rendered literally,—whether, in short, it is poetical to write of arms, hands, and feet. I do not see why these, if beautiful, should not be introduced as well as hair, eyes, and face. I maintain that it is the duty of the translator to be as literal as possible, notwithstanding Voltaire's anathema, "Malheur aux faiseurs de traductions littérales;—c'est là qu'on peut dire que la lettre tue." D'Alembert gives the translator great license when he says,—"Correct the defective traits of the original, and suppress superfluous accessories which the rhyme exacts and which add nothing to the force of the thought." But, with all submission, I contend that to do this effectually is to make the translator a greater man than his master. The directions may apply to French translators of Petrarch; for, as the Abbé de Sade remarks, "Le poète Italian ploie sa langue à son génie; le Français est contraint de ployer son génie à sa langue."[1]

---

[1] The translations of Petrarch's sonnets into French verse by De Sade cannot take rank among *Les Belles Infidèles* referred to by Count Simeon (*Horace*, traduction en vers, Paris, 1873),—"On les amait pour leur beauté, on les fuyait pour leur trahison." The

But in translating from Italian into English, the main object ought to be to represent the original as faithfully as the form, the constraint of rhyme and metre, and the necessity of employing poetical language will allow. In the case before us, I confess to a preference of the catalogue of Laura's charms as given by Petrarch, to the mode in which the translators referred to, attempt to get over the supposed objection. One speaks of "the limbs of heavenly mould;" another of "the taper arms," and in thus correcting "the defective parts of the original," actually omits two whole lines of his author, and inserts his own nonsense, such as, "the heavenly mould of that angelic form," and "those eyes whose living lustre shed the heat of bright meridian day,"—not a word of which is in Petrarch's sonnet, and one would be ashamed of him if it were. Another says that by these charms our poet was "parted from the vulgar and the vain." This is a wonderful mode of improving on one's author. The shrinking timidity of Petrarch made him feel

Abbé's translations have no beauty, but much treason. He disregards the structure and limits of the sonnet, sometimes extending it to upwards of twenty lines, at other times reducing it to ten or twelve. In a note appended to his version of the 26th Sonnet, he says naively:—"A la description du matin, contenue dans les premiers vers, Pétrarque ajoute une image que j'ai supprimée parce qu'elle ne m'a pas paru assez noble."

Count Simeon well describes the success of modern translation as "Cette lutte entre deux idiomes, l'un resistant à l'autre, mais à la fin dompté, sans être ni asservi ni avili."

that he was unlike other men, and he fancied he read in other men's looks their consciousness of his singularity,—

E fatto singular dell' altra genti.
And make me appear strange to other people.

Such are the dangers that beset the translator who flatters himself that he can improve on a better man than himself.

38. Much of the freshness of Petrarch's poetry arises from his habit of jotting down his thoughts as they occurred to him in his solitary wanderings amongst the lovely or wild scenery of the retreat which he often sought (20). But in view of the elaborate care with which he revised his work, it might be supposed that his language is intricate and subtle. So far from this being the case, his language is most simple, and his meaning most direct. He goes straight to his object and clothes it in the simplest words, and with little or no inversion. His sparing use of adjectives is also remarkable; these are left to their own suggestion; and when he does make use of them, they are felt to be necessary, because they are appropriate. Combined with all this simplicity of language is a fullness of meaning, and a breadth and completeness of effect, which produce the result of a highly-finished whole; and such is the ease and grace of all his

best sonnets, that the labour of revision is never apparent.[1] I do not intend to apply these remarks to every sonnet. A man could not write upwards of three hundred such poems and produce the same result in all. But I do not know of a single sonnet that does not repay the reader, if not the translator; for there is always to be found a sweet thought, tenderly and elegantly expressed, charming the sense by its beauty, and pleasing the fancy by its novelty,—and this even in the midst of exaggeration which falls on the ear like bombast. Of course in so long and celebrated a series, some of its terms stand out in pre-eminent beauty, and one of these may be selected in order to show, by contrast, some of the various modes in which it has been handled by translators. I give the original, and then my own translation, thus affording other writers in this rich field the means of applying to me the tests I am about to apply to them; as it is possible that, while being sensitive to the defects of others, I am not sufficiently conscious of my own.

[1] Matthew Arnold, in his three Oxford lectures "On Translating Homer" (1861), remarks that the translator must be permeated by four qualities of his author :—(1.) Homer is eminently rapid ; (2.) He is eminently plain and direct in the evolution of his thought and in its expression, that is, both in his syntax and his words ; (3.) He is eminently plain and direct in the substance of his thought, that is, in his matter and ideas ; and (4.) He is eminently noble. These four qualities also apply to Dante and Petrarch, and must be recognised on the part of their translator.

Sonnet XXVIII. Type I. } *Solo, e pensoso, etc.*

Solo e pensoso i più deserti campi
Vo misurando a passi tardi e lenti;
E gli occhi porto, per fuggir, intenti,
Dove vestigio uman l 'arena stampi.
Altro schermo non trovo, che mi scampi
Dal manifesto accorger delle genti:
Perchè negli atti d 'allegrezza spenti
Di fuor si legge, com' io dentro avvampi:
Si ch' io mi credo omai, che monti, e piagge,
E fiumi, e selve sappian di che tempre
Sia la mia vita, ch' è celata altrui.
Ma pur si aspre vie, nè si selvagge
Cercar non so, ch' amor non venga sempre
Ragionando con meco, ed io con lui.

Alone and pensive, the most desert land
  I measure o'er with loitering steps and slow;
  Gazing around me, that I may not go
  Where trace of human footsteps marks the sand.
No other refuge have I at command,
  From idler's recognition; for I know
  I bear the outward marks of inward woe;
  Of joys consumed by Love's unsparing hand.
So that I now believe my life's sad mood
  Is known to woods and streams, to hill and plain,
  The life that I from others would conceal:
I know not where to find a wild rough road,
  But Love to me will always access gain,
  And he to me, and I to him appeal.

Three translations of this sonnet are given in Bohn's collection; the first of which is signed "Anon. Ox. 1795;" the second "I. B. Taylor;" and the third "Macgregor." In the first of these the concluding lines of the second quatrain are thus rendered—

> "So well my wild disordered gestures show
> And love-lorn looks, the fire within me bred."

If one sonnet of Petrarch more than another requires simplicity of treatment, it is this: but to deal with it thus in the spirit of modern pastoral poetry is to produce an insipid, if not a nauseous result.

The second translation is in the same style—

> "While in my hollow cheek and haggard eye
> Appears the fire that burns my inmost heart."

The third translation is perhaps the worst of the three—

> "Lest on my brow, a stranger long to joy,
> He read the secret fire which makes my pain."

In the first line of the second quatrain, this translator has

> "No help save this I find, some cave to gain."

There is nothing about seeking a cave in the original, and nothing to suggest it.

39. It is natural that a translator should find fault with the labours of his predecessors, if only to justify his own work and the need of a fresh effort. I have taken about twenty-five of Petrarch's most celebrated sonnets and compared them with the various translations given in Bohn's collection. The conclusion I have arrived at, from this comparison, is that Petrarch has not hitherto been properly rendered into English. The poet Campbell "despaired of ever seeing in English verse a translation of Petrarch's Italian poetry that shall be adequate and popular. The term adequate, of course, always applies to the translation of genuine poetry in a subdued sense. It means the best that can be expected, after making allowance for that escape of ethereal spirit which is inevitable in the transfer of poetic thought from one language to another. The word popular is also to be taken in a limited meaning regarding all translations." Cowper's Homer is not so popular as his John Gilpin; but Cowper's Homer and Cary's Dante are, in Campbell's opinion, both adequate and popular; but no translation of Petrarch can be such, because the translator cannot "transfer into English those graces of Petrarchan diction which are mostly intransferable." Hence arises the proposition that Petrarch is not so genuine a poet as Homer or Dante, "since his charm depends upon the delicacies of diction that evaporate in the transfer from

tongue to tongue, more than on hardy thoughts that will take root in any language to which they are transplanted." If such a conclusion be based upon existing published translations, judging from the specimens I have examined, my contention is that such translations do not represent the poet fairly: they are not "the best that can be expected;" they are not the best that can be produced, and I proceed to justify this assertion by examples in which my intention is to prove that published translations frequently contain (*a*) positive mistranslations, arising apparently from an inadequate knowledge of the Italian language on the part of the translator, so that on comparing translations by different hands, one may contradict the other; (*b*) paraphrases or the substitution of the translator's ideas for those of the poet; (*c*) inelegant unpoetical English; (*d*) the general absence of any attempt to reproduce the simple language of the poet where simple language in English is possible; (*e*) want of attention to the form and metrical arrangement of the original. Some sonnets are even translated into blank verse, and others into the forms adopted by Shakspere and Spenser.

SONNET CCCXIII.

I quai posi in amar cosa mortale.
"In vain idolatry of mortal things."

Sheppard.

Cosa mortale is "a mortal thing," and that is Laura.

Sonnet CCLII.

Or vorrei ben piacer : ma quella altera
Tacito stanco dopo se mi chiama.

"Fain would I now taste joy; but that high fair,
Silent and weary, calls me to her there."
Macgregor.

The idea is lost in this rendering. The poet has just said that if he had supposed his verses would have given so much pleasure, he would have taken more pains with them; that he wrote not for fame, but to relieve his trouble; but now, he says, that "the desire to please is come, I am mute and weary, and she on high calls me to her."

Wollaston's translation is nearer the original, but does not express it properly—

"And could the world's fair suffrage now be bought
'Twere joy to gain; but that my hour is brief,
Her lofty spirit waves me to her bier."

This is wanting in the simplicity and directness of the original. Wollaston employs fourteen words for Petrarch's four; omits the sad and expressive words "mute and weary;" and introduces "bier," which is anti-Petrarchan, for the poet regards Laura as a living beatified spirit.

Sonnet II.

Era la mia virtute al cor ristretta,
Per far ivi, e negli occhi sue difese :

"My courage had retired within my heart,
 There to defend the pass bright eyes might gain."
Nott.

"My virtue had retired to watch my heart,
 Thence of weak eyes the danger to repel."
Macgregor.

They cannot both be right: bright eyes and weak eyes.

Sonnet CLXXV.

*Ch' i' non vo' dir di lei; ma chi la scorge,
 Tutto 'l cor di dolcezza, e d' amor l'empie;
 Tanto n' ha seco, e tant' altrui ne porge:*

"Let me not speak of her, but him her guide,
 Who all her heart with love and sweetness fills—
 Gifts which from him o'erflowing follow her."
Macgregor.

A complete misunderstanding; although the translator throws off the shackles of rhyme, and renders this difficult sonnet in blank verse. The real sense is, I believe, as follows:—" I wish not to speak of her; but whoever looks at her, she fills his whole heart with sweetness and with love; she being so richly endowed with these qualities herself, that she lavishes them upon others." I admit the difficulty of rendering these three Italian lines into a similar number of English heroic verses, and yet retain the sense and the poetry; but if an attempt be made at all, such ought to be the result.

Sonnet CCXCI.

There is a piece of delicate satire in one of the lines of this sonnet, which the translator has missed altogether. The poet describes Nature as having heaped all her gifts of beauty on Laura, and he closes the second quatrain thus—

Perdonimi qual è bella, o si tene

(Pardon me, whoever is beautiful or esteems herself to be so.)

The translator above referred to renders the line thus—

"Ladies, your pardon let my boldness claim."

It does not seem very difficult to retain the wit as well as the sense of this line, something after this fashion—

Pardon, ye fair! or ye who think ye're fair!

Sonnet LXXX.

La voglia e la ragion combattut 'hanno
   Sette, e sett' anni; e vincerà il migliore;
   S'anime son quaggiù del ben presaghe.

"For fourteen years did reason proudly fling
   Defiance at my tameless will, to win
   A triumph blest, if man can good foretell."
                               Wollaston.

This does not express the meaning; nor is it Petrarchan language in the Lauran sonnets to talk about proudly flinging defiance. The poet was too conscious of his own weakness to sing in this boastful strain, and the idea expressed in this tercet is in harmony with his other sonnets. Here he represents Passion and Reason as equal foes: they have now been contending during fourteen years, and his hope is that the more virtuous force will prevail, if the mind here below can foresee its own good.

Sonnet LXIX.

Io che l'esca amorosa al petto avea,
Qual maraviglia, se di subit 'arsi.

"I whose whole breast with Love's soft food was sown,
What wonder if at once my bosom glow'd?"

Anon. Ox. 1795.

The Italian is, "I, who had amorous tinder at my breast, what marvel if it suddenly kindled?" This is a complete figure; but we cannot suppose "Love's soft food" (whatever that may be) sown all over the breast, to produce a conflagration.

Sonnet CXIII.

Ponmi, ove 'l Sol occide i fiori e l'erba;
O dove vince lui 'l ghiaccio e la neve:

"Place me where herb and flower the sun has dried,
Or where numb winter's grasp holds sterner sway."

Dacre.

Surely the simple and direct statements of the original are more vigorous than this translation. "Place me where the sun kills the flowers and the grass, or where the ice and snow o'ercome him." Why talk about "numb Winter," or holding "sterner sway"? Perhaps it may be said that this is poetry, and that mine is prose. But the prose is easily put into verse. In a translation marked "*Anon.* 1777," the two lines are thus rendered—

"Place me where Phœbus burns each herb, each flower,
Or where cold snows and frost o'ercome his rays."

This is better than the former; but why "*cold snows and frost*"? The couplet is, however, sufficiently good to be made better, and the following is, I think, better:—

Place me where Sol burns up the grass and flower,
Or where the ice and snow o'ercome his rays.

Take another line from the same sonnet—

Ponmi alla notte, al di lungo, ed al breve
"Place me where blind night rules or lengthened day."
Dacre.

The Italian is

Place me in night, in long or in short days.

Or, again,

Ponm' in cielo, od in terra, od in abisso.
"Place me in heaven, or in the abyss profound."
Dacre.

An abyss is naturally profound—then why say so? and why omit "on earth"? Why not say—
>Place me in heaven, on earth, or in the abyss?

Sonnet CCXLI.

Sol un riposo trovo in molti affanni;
Che, quando torni, ti conosco e 'ntendo
All' andar, alla voce, al volto, a' panni.
"No balm relieves the anguish I endure,
Save the fond feeble hope that thou art near
To soothe my sufferings with an angel's tear."
Bannerman.

A paraphrase like this, in which the translator's ideas take the place of the author's, resembles those intricate variations on some popular air, in which the original melody is altogether lost. The melody itself may be sweet and touching, and even bring tears to the eyes; but the variations never do so; and when a translator makes his author say what the translator thinks he ought to have said, but did not, not only is the sense of the original lost, but there is this danger, that the style of the variations may be quite opposed to the style of the author. The above passage, literally rendered, is as follows:

"One only comfort I find in many troubles—that when thou returnest [to Vaucluse] I seem to recognise and understand thee by thy walk, thy voice, thy face, and thy dress."

Sonnet CXLIII. Second Quatrain.

E vo cantando (o penser miei non saggi!)
Lei ch 'l ciel non poria lontana farme:

> *Ch' i l' ho negli occhi, e veder seco parme*
> *Donne, e donzelle; e sono abeti, e faggi.*

The poet is travelling through the forest of Ardennes on his way from Cologne to Vaucluse, "and goes singing (O thoughts! not wise) of her whom heaven cannot keep far from my mind; so that I not only have her image in my eyes, but see with her a number of dames and damsels; and yet they are only beeches and pines." In a translation, dated *Anon.* 1777, this quatrain is thus rendered—

> "Often I sing, all thoughtless as I stray."

[He was anything but thoughtless: and he was not straying; for in one of his letters he relates that while pushing on through the gloomy and, at that time, dangerous forest, the Twenty-third Psalm came into his mind so forcibly that he repeated aloud the verse, "Yea, though I walk through the valley of the shadow of death, I will fear no evil,—for thou art with me; thy rod and thy staff they comfort me." He then went on to think how that Laura also was always present to him, and he composed this sonnet, *Per mezz' i boschi inospiti e selvaggi*, a translation of which is given in Part II. But to return to our criticism.]

> "Of her I sing, all thoughtless as I stray,
>   Whose sweet idea strong as heaven's shall prove;
>   And oft methinks these pines and beeches move
>   Like nymphs—'mid which fond fancy sees her play."

This really seems to me to be nothing more nor less than a distortion of the original. Nor is Macgregor's version an improvement on the above:—

"Singing fond thoughts in simple lays to her,
 Whom time and space so little hide from me;
 E'en here her form, nor hers alone, I see
 But maids and matrons in each beech and fir."

The anonymous translator seems also to have missed the idea of the concluding tercet of this sonnet.

Raro un silenzio, un solitario orrore
 D'ombrosa selva mai tanto mi piacque;
 Se non che del mio Sol troppo si perde.

"The unusual silence and solitary horror of this dark wood" [how graphic are these few words in the original!] "ever pleased me; only too much of my sun is lost in it." That is, as the dark wood excludes the light of the sun, so it also excludes the light of Laura's eyes. The conceit is forced and unnatural; but it is not well expressed in the following translation:—

"How grateful might this darksome wood appear
 Where horror reigns, where scarce a sound is heard,
 But ah! 'tis far from all my heart holds dear."

Sonnet CLXXVIII.

Sotti biondi capei canuta mente,
 E'n umil donna alta beltà divina:

"Experienced judgment with fair hair combined,
 High heavenly beauty in a humble fair."

Macgregor.

This reads very much like a parody. It must be admitted, however, that the original is so marked by sweetness and simplicity that it is difficult to render it in English without being puerile—

>'Neath auburn tresses a most candid mind
>Beauty divine in humble modest guise.

In the same sonnet the verse

>*Ch' ogni dur rompe, ed ogni altezza inchina,*

is thus translated—

>"The hard to break, the high and haughty tear,"

that is, Laura's vivacious wit overcomes both the hard-hearted and the proud,—but it does not tear them.

>*E torre l' alme a' corpi, e darle altrui.*

Laura's eyes have such power that they can sever the soul from one body and give it to another. But the translator says that her eyes

>"take
>Souls from our bodies and their own to make."

Laura's talk is said to be sweetly interrupted by her sighs

>*Con i sospir soavemente rotti,*

but the translator has—

>"Evermore broken by the balmiest sighs."

Petrarch is very choice in the use of adjectives, and, where it is possible, avoids them altogether. He takes it for granted that all Laura's attributes are fair, lovely, beautiful, etc.; and does not trouble himself to say so; but his delicate sense of the beautiful often leads him to throw the adjective into the adverbial form, which, in conjunction with verbs and participles, has a charming effect, as in the case before us. Now, unless the translator pays some attention to the principles which guided the poet in his versification, it is impossible to give any idea of the delicate beauty of the original. That the English language is capable of sweetness is abundantly proved by our own poets. Spenser, when he imitates Tasso, and also when he writes on his own account, can command sweet and tender language as the occasion requires. But our translators of Petrarch seem to go out of their way to avoid sweetness of expression, when the original seems to compel it. It cannot be unreasonable to expect that the same mode of treatment adopted by Petrarch ought to be the standard for the translator so far as the different structures of the two languages allow.

In the exquisitely simple tercet already referred to (36)—

> *Non sa com' Amor sana, e come ancide,*
> *Chi non sa come dolce ella sospira,*
> *E come dolce parla, e dolce ride.*

> He knows not how Love heals, or how Love slays,
>   Who knows not how she sweetly, sweetly sighs,
>   And how she sweetly speaks and sweetly smiles.

In Dr. Nott's translation, the adverbs are converted into adjectives, which is opposed to Petrarch's manner—

> " How Love can heal his wounds, then wound again,
>   He only knows, who knows how sweet her sighs,
>   How sweet her converse, and how sweet her smile."

Even the poet Campbell fails, I think, to reproduce the simple beauty of the original—

> "He knows not Love who has not seen her eyes,
>   Turn when she sweetly speaks, or smiles or sighs,
>   Or how the power of love can hurt or heal."

In the tercet preceding this, Petrarch has the same beautiful simplicity of handling—

> *Per divina bellezza indarno mira,*
>   *Chi gli òcchi di costei giammai non vide,*
>   *Come soavemente ella gli gira.*

" He looks in vain for divine beauty who never sees the eyes of this one: how sweetly she turns them." Now see how this is amplified, and, as I think, spoiled, in another translation :—

> "For heavenly beauty he in vain inquires,
>   Who ne'er beheld her eyes' celestial stain,
>   Where'er she turns around their brilliant fires."

This is not to translate Petrarch. He uses the quiet

expression "her eyes," not "her eyes' celestial stain," whatever that may mean, by the side of "brilliant fires," about which Petrarch says nothing.

If, as I complain, the translations hitherto published fail to give an adequate idea of Petrarch's sweetness and simplicity, they do not seem to me to succeed in properly rendering his strength and power. In that wonderful sonnet (CV.) in which he denounces the corrupt papal court of Avignon, the last line is

Or vivi si, ch 'a Dio ne venga il lezzo.

Thy life is such—its stench ascends to God.

This is strong language; the poet meant it to be such. But Dr. Nott tames it down into

"Now rank to heaven ascends thy life unclean."

And this is not only tame but inaccurate, for how can an unclean life ascend to heaven? Wyatt's translation is much more vigorous, and therefore to the purpose—

"That it dothe stinke before the face of God."

Sonnet VII.

Povera e nuda vai, Filosofia.

In the translation of this sonnet, dated *Anon.* 1777, this simple verse is thus rendered—

"Let want, let shame, philosophy attend."

Whereas the poet simply states a fact—

"Philosophy! thou goest poor and naked."

This is like Juvenal's *Probitas laudatur et alget*—a simple statement that honesty is praised and neglected; but no one would think of saying "Let honesty be praised and starved."

Sonnet CCCVII.

e tanta luce
Dentr 'al mio core infin dal Ciel traluce,
Ch' i' 'ncomincio a contar il tempo, e i danni.

"So rare a light and true
Shines e'en from heaven my secret conscience through,
Of lost time and loved sin the glass it rears."
Macgregor.

The original is—

And so much heaven-born light illumines my heart, that I begin to take account of time and its losses.

I am not aware that any apology is needed on my part for finding so much fault with the labours of my predecessors; but the more closely I examine them, the more often do they seem to have been wilfully deaf to the magic of Petrarch's lute, or how could they have preferred their own dissonance? And yet many of these translations are distinguished by well-known names. Charlotte Smith, for instance, attained to some poetical celebrity in her time; nevertheless, she has so handled a few of

Petrarch's sonnets as to make them no longer recognisable. For example, in the 238th sonnet, the spirit of Laura appears to the poet and bids him not to weep for her, for when she ceased to be mortal she became immortal :—

> And when death seemed to close my eyes in night,
> I opened them in the eternal light.

Instead of this remarkable expression of thought, we find the following piece of sentimentality :—

> "Ah! yield not thus to culpable despair,
> But raise thy eyes to heaven, and think I wait thee there!"

This sonnet opens with so much freshness and beauty, that we may fancy ourselves with the poet in Vaucluse.

> What time birds pipe their plaint, and every tree
> Its green arms rustles in the summer air;
> And on the fresh and flowery banks, to me,
> Comes the hoarse murmur of the waters clear,
> Pensive I write of Love while seated here.

This is as literal as I can make it, and it seems just as easy to follow the author as to write in such a strain as this :—

> "Where the green leaves exclude the summer beam,
> And softly bend as balmy breezes blow,
> And where, with liquid lapse, the lucid stream,
> Across the fretted rock is heard to flow,
> Pensive I lay."

Who would suppose that these fragments refer to corresponding passages of the same sonnet?

If the author had given these lines in a poem of her own, it would, of course, be impertinent to object to them; but as in my copy of her poems (Tenth edition, 1811) Sonnet XV. is headed "From Petrarch," I am bound to treat it as a translation; especially as she gives the first line of the sonnet in a note, *Se lamentar augelli*, etc., and is careful to distinguish another sonnet from the Italian as not being "meant as a translation."

The first tercet of the 283d sonnet contains such good poetry that I should despair of giving the reader any idea of it, except by earnestly endeavouring to be as close to the original as possible; and even then, I fail to give the touching accents of the poet. I also add the second tercet for the sake of the comparison I am about to make.

> O beauteous lady! thou hast slept brief sleep,
>   And waking, found thyself 'mong spirits blest,
>   Thy soul with the soul's Maker recombined:
> And if my rhymes have any power to keep
>   A place among the noblest minds and best,
>   Thy mem'ry is to immortal fame consigned.

In a translation of this sonnet by Mr. Morehead, these tercets are thus rendered:—

> " He," that is Love,
> " He tells me, lady, that one moment's sleep

Alone was thine, and then thou didst awake
Among the elect, and in thy Maker's arms :
And if my verse Oblivion's power can keep
Aloof, thy name its place on earth will take
Where genius still will dote upon thy charms."

The touching words of Laura in the 261st sonnet—

Lo ! I am she who caused thee strife and pain,
And closed my day before the eve was near :

are made to assume this awkward style by Wrangham—

"I, I am she, thy breast with slights who tore,
And ere its evening closed my day's brief space."

40. I could add to these examples to almost any extent, but must now end my ungracious task, in the full assurance that the motive that suggested it will not be misunderstood. There is, however, one more source of error which has led some translators astray, and that is the adoption of the language of gallantry, such as "my fair one's radiant eyes," "the cruel she," "none but herself can be her parallel," "she too of loveliest face, for whom I burn;" and many other similar passages to be found in the English versions of Petrarch's sonnets. To write thus is to misunderstand the deep feeling of reverence and even adoration with which the poet regards Laura. He expresses all the doubts and fears, the hopes and desires of an ardent lover; but

he never acts the fine gentleman or the gallant towards her; he expresses his torments, but is never trivial or condescending or patronising; he worships a being who is too beautiful in his estimation for this earth, and who is endowed with the graces of heaven. The following specimen may serve to some extent to illustrate these remarks.

SONNET CLXXXIV. } *Onde tolse Amor l'oro, e*
TYPE I. } *di qual vena.*

Say! from what mine did Love the gold supply
   To make those auburn tresses? from what tree
   Culled he the roses? Whence, too, gathered he
Fresh, tender rime? and these all vivify?
And whence the pearls, that guide and modify
   Words, flowing sweet and rare, in purity?
   Whence can so many heavenly beauties be
Of that dear face, serener than the sky?
What angels lent their aid, or what high sphere,
   To that celestial song, that moves me so
   That I no more command a tranquil mind?
What sun produced the lustre, pure and clear,
   Of those bright eyes, whence strife and peace I know,
   Fire in my heart and icy fetters find?

Although the foregoing be but a faint reflection of the beauty of the original, it will show the reader how the poet addressed Laura during her life. Many other examples are given in these pages, from which it appears that his admiration is always tempered with deep reverence; a feeling that must exclude the *petit-maître*, no less than the modern pastoral poet, whose verses are so insipid, because the inspiration is not real. The same intense adoration, also, almost entirely excluded the heathen gods and goddesses from Petrarch's poems, to the no small relief of the reader; and it will readily be understood that, in the poet's estimation, Laura far excelled Venus and the Graces both in person and mind; so that there was no place for them in his poems. Moreover, as already remarked (33), Petrarch had his own peculiar views as to the scope and object of classical poetry,—he judged that it ought to stand by itself; and that modern poetry, to be worthy of the name, ought also to have its own distinctive features, which, while separating it from the classics, ought at the same time to be capable of commanding the respect and admiration of cultivated modern taste. Dante and Boccaccio held similar views, and, assisted by our own Chaucer (who loved Petrarch, and translated one of his sonnets) (32), the foundations of modern literature were laid on a firm basis.

If Laura, in the full flush of health and loveliness, inspired such beautiful poetry, her illness leads to outpourings equally beautiful, as in the following sonnet, which Petrarch composed after calling to take leave of her on his way to Italy.

SONNET CCXI. } *Qual paura ho, quando mi*
TYPE I.   *torna a mente.*

What anguish mine that day remembering well,
  On which I bade adieu to her most dear;
  She pensive, grave: my heart I left with her;
  I often love to think of that farewell!
Methinks I see her, as it then befell,
  Stand meekly circled round by women fair,
  Like to a rose, 'midst other flowers less rare:
  Nor gay nor sad; as dreading unfelt ill.
Her wonted ornaments all laid aside,
  The pearls, the garlands, and the dress so gay,
  The smile, the song, the sympathising speech;
I quitted life in quitting her loved side,
  Assailed by dark forebodings, dreams, dismay:
  God grant these ills the loved one never reach!

After Laura's death, the poet's feelings became still more impassioned and intensified, so that it is impossible to mistake their meaning. He is grateful to her for her seeming coolness which preserved both him and her pure. She is now in heaven interceding for him, watching over him, sympathising with him, consoling him in his dreams, conversing with him with all the tenderness of a mother to her child, or devoted wife to her husband. No saint was ever adored with such fervour; or addressed in such beautiful impassioned language. Here are two specimens:—

SONNET CCLIV.
Second Variation of the Quatrains. Tercets as in Type I.

Soleano i miei pensier soavemente.

My thoughts were wont in many a sweet-toned lay,
   To hold discourse on her for whom those tears :
   Now Pity comes, repenting her delay,
   Perchance she speaks of me, or hopes, or fears.
But since she closed on earth those fleeting years,
   Since the last hour of that her final day ;
   She from her heavenly seat feels, sees, and hears,
   My state—this only solace can convey.
O gentle miracle ! O spirit blest !
   O beauty unexampled, high and rare !
   Too soon to seek the source from whence it came !
The world to make her good deeds manifest ;
   Gives crown and palm :—fame, too, in accents clear,
   Lauds her excelling virtues, and my flame.

SONNET CCCVIII.
TYPE I.

Non può far morte il dolce viso amaro.

Death could not mar the sweetness of that face,
   But that sweet face made Death e'en sweet appear ;
   So that, in dying, I have nought to fear,
   But follow her in whom all good I trace :
And HIM who, for our sakes, sought Death's embrace,
   Whose foot burst the Tartarean portal drear ;
   So that His dying comes my soul to cheer ;
   Then welcome Death ! thy advent brings me peace.

My time is come: oh why so long delay?
  For if thy dart is not prepared, then know,
  I was prepared when she gave up her breath.
From then till now, I have not lived a day:
  With her I lived; with her I felt thy blow,
  My day becomes (her journey ended) death.

41. Having in the course of these remarks given a number of examples of Petrarch's love sonnets, at least so far as my translations serve to convey them, I may close this part of my subject with a specimen of the poet's indignant style. He was intimately acquainted with the manners of the Papal Court at Avignon, and writes this and a few other sonnets in the same fearless tone.

SONNET CV. } *Fiamma del ciel sulle tue trecce*
TYPE II. }   *piova.*

Heaven's flame, thou sinner! on thy tresses rain,
  Who, scorning bread and water, once thy fare,
  Grow'st rich and great by making others bare,
  Since from each evil act thou gettest gain.
Thou nest of treasons! hatching every sin,
  That now spreads o'er the world its baneful snare;
  Wine, lust, excess, thee for their slave declare;
  To luxury's topmost point thou dost attain.
Old men and damsels through thy chambers glide,
  In wanton glee, each sin obscene the mode,
  And vanity, Beelzebub the guide.
Thou wast not reared in sloth; for thou hast trod,
  Barefoot, rough ways; naked, the wind defied:
  Thy life is such—its stench ascends to God.

42. In conclusion, I would remark that if Petrarch has made but little impression on the English reader, it is, according to my view, because he has not been properly translated. In attempting to justify this opinion by an examination of published translations, I have selected examples from the best sonnets as being calculated to try the powers of the translator most severely; and if they have in so many instances failed to give a proper account of their author, then there seems to be room for fresh efforts. If poetry be " impassioned truth," we have it in Petrarch. If poetry consist of " man's thoughts tinged by his feelings," we have poetry in these sonnets; and it is not too much to require of the translator that he be able to bring to his work something of the same power that inspired his author. It is not enough that a man be well read in literature, clever and accomplished; he must be something of a poet, or he will fail to detect the subtle delicacy and beauty of such a genius as Petrarch. I say this with a full conviction that my own work is far from being perfect, and I am free to admit that it is more easy to rouse one's energies to an analysis of the defects of others, than to set about correcting one's own.

43. At the same time, I am satisfied that the business of the translator is not an elegant employment for ladies and gentlemen " who write with ease," and fancy they have done their work when

they have loosely and inaccurately reproduced something of their author, in smooth verses, with a certain arrangement of rhymes. Translation worthy of the name implies, as all good work does, hard work, assisted by a proper amount of knowledge of the subject in hand. And this hard work cannot be accomplished at one sitting. The conscientious translator of Petrarch will be glad to take a lesson from his master, and we have already gained some idea of his mode of working (19). He was in the habit of sketching out a sonnet, as the thought occurred to him, there and then; not pausing to place the right word in the right place, but caring only to lay down the framework of the structure; to secure the thought while still on the wing and within range; submitting himself to the inspiration of the time and the place; and by his first rough sketch securing the truth and freshness that marks all work that derives its inspiration from nature. He then laid the sketch aside, and at his leisure took it up and studied it, putting in here a new word and there another, or writing over one word two or three others for future choice. We know from Ubaldini's publication of Petrarch's MS. corrections (19) that he did this repeatedly and often at long intervals of time, and it was not until after constant repetitions of this *labor limæ* that he dismissed the sonnet as a finished production. Not that he even now regarded it as perfect; for he has told us that had he known that his Italian poems would have become so popular, he would have bestowed still more pains upon them (28). Here, then, we see how a great mind works—the inspiration of the time and place is due to nature, the elaboration, the workmanlike result, is due to art; and all this may serve as a useful lesson to every one engaged in any intellectual pursuit.

44. The business of the translator is an intellectual pursuit. He must supersaturate himself with his author; study him night and day, not only in the works that are the object of translation, but in his life and habits, in his letters and correspondence, so as to obtain light from the author himself as to his purpose and meaning in a particular composition. And if all this is necessary in the case of most authors that we propose to translate, it is especially so in the case of Petrarch; for he carried on a brisk correspondence, and inserted in his letters a multitude of personal details which throw light upon his works. Had some of the translators that I have ventured to criticise done this, they could not have fallen into certain of the errors that have been pointed out (39). They could not, for example, have said that the poet was singing "all thoughtless as I stray," when the sonnet itself says no such thing; and one of the poet's letters tells us that he was in a most earnest frame of mind when he composed it. They could not

write "straying," had they known that he was pushing on through a dangerous forest in war time.

45. When Petrarch in his youth inquired of a learned friend what was the best kind of knowledge to acquire in order to become a poet, the answer was "Learn everything!" So we may say to the translator, "Learn all you can about your author, and the subject on which he writes."

46. But the point before us is how to translate one of Petrarch's sonnets. There are times when the spirit of the poet seems to be hovering over the translator, superintending the transmutation of his own work. Then it is that the lines seem to translate themselves, and the translation reflects much of the grace and freedom of the original. But such occasions are rare; and, in general, the translator, like an ordinary mortal, has to confine his powers within the limits of mechanical rules. Taking one of Petrarch's sonnets, for example, the translator must—*First*, understand it in the original Italian, and this, as we have seen, is not always easy without collateral aid, however simple the language may appear. *Secondly*, He must translate the sonnet in the rough, making it as smooth as possible at one sitting, and then put it aside. *Thirdly*, When so disposed he is to look at the translation, compare it with the original, and endeavour to improve it. This process is to be repeated many times. I know that I have often dismissed with complacency the

rendering of a sonnet, and thought myself a clever fellow for doing it so well; but on taking it up a week afterwards, or reading it over with a friend well versed in Petrarchan lore, all my self-conceit vanished, and it became evident that the file had to be used again and again with patient industry.

Any one who can command sufficient self-denial to undertake such labour, soon becomes aware of several advantages resulting from it. He improves his style in composition, cultivates his critical faculty, and elevates his poetical tastes and sympathy; he also learns how to work out a thought with logical brevity and accuracy. With a view to these advantages, I would recommend the sonnet not only to the young translator, but also to those who write what is called "original poetry." The wholesome limits imposed by this small poem tend to check diffuseness whether in thought or expression; and also to encourage the idea that the sonnet, like a small cabinet picture which the eye can take in at a glance, ought to be highly finished.

47. Taking it for granted that the object of all this care is to make a faithful translation, the translator will not obtrude himself, but rather sink himself in his author. And in addition to the collateral aid just referred to, he will seek assistance from commentators, who, in the case of Petrarch, are numerous. There are between three and four hundred editions of Petrarch's Italian poems, a large

number of which are annotated. However it may be the fashion to despise commentators, it may be conceded, at least in the case before us, that they know more of their author than we do; that as Italians of culture, they could explain the poet's meaning much more fully and correctly than we can pretend to do; and hence are fully entitled to our respect and regard. Now I venture to affirm that not one of the numerous translations given in Bohn's collection derived any assistance from the Italian commentators, or many of the errors pointed out would not have been perpetrated. Passing over obvious errors arising from deficient knowledge of the Italian, or loose paraphrases which came into fashion with Pope's so-called translation of Homer, let us take an example in which most English scholars, with a competent knowledge of Italian, would be likely to fall into error without the assistance of a native comment. In the 241st sonnet, the poet expresses his gratitude to the spirit of Laura for visiting him and consoling him; and her image is so distinctly brought out before him, while wandering about the Vaucluse valley, that he says—

> *Cosi incomincio a ritrovar presenti*
> *Le tue bellezze a' suo' usati soggiorni.*

Now almost every Italian scholar would translate these two lines thus :—

"So that I begin to find again before me thy charms in their accustomed sojourn."

And in two published translations this rendering is adopted. The first, by Wrangham, runs thus:—

"Thus do I seem again to trace below
Thy beauties hovering o'er their loved sojourn."

The second is by Anne Bannerman—

"Methinks I meet thee in each former scene,
Once the sweet shelter of a heart serene."

Now the commentator Tassoni has a special note on this passage. He says that by *usati soggiorni* "the poet means the appropriate localities of female beauties, such as the colour of the hair, the lustre of the eyes, the redness of the lips," etc. Zotti also makes a similar comment. He says that *a' suoi usati soggiorni* implies "in the same places where the poet was accustomed to see them, namely, on the cheeks the roses, in the teeth the whiteness, in the eyes the vivacity, etc."

But should the translators object to this view on the ground that the very next line to this passage defines a topographical locality—

La 've cantando andai de te molt 'anni.

(There where I was wont during many years to sing of thee.)

—the answer is, that so far from this being an argument in their favour, it is directly opposed to them. So excellent a master of the sonnet as Petrarch would be likely in the first line of the first tercet, which this is, to break new ground, and not simply continue the same idea from the second quatrain, and that this was also Zotti's opinion is proved by the fact that he has a note on the line *La 've*, etc., "that is, in Vaucluse."

Another curious example may be given. On his first journey to Rome the poet landed in Tuscany, and one of the first objects that met his view was a laurel. This recalled Laura so forcibly to his mind that he rushed to gather it, not seeing in his way a stream covered with verdure, into which he fell. This accident led to the production of the 51st sonnet, *Del mar Tirreno*, etc., in which the above facts are related, and the moral is thus given in the second tercet:—

> *Piacemi almen d'aver cangiato stile*
> *Dagli occhi a' piè; se del lor esser molli*
> *Gli altri asciugasse un più cortese Aprile.*

"At least I am pleased to have changed my style from eyes to feet"—that is, his style had hitherto produced wet eyes—it now produces wet feet. "And it would please me well, if by reason of being wet in the feet, a more gracious April would dry my eyes [*gli altri*]." From which we learn that the accident took place in April, the month of tears or showers; and as the April sun dried his feet, so might a more propitious April (Laura) dry his eyes.

These three lines being thus so full of meaning, a translator must necessarily fail unless he makes himself acquainted with all the conditions under which they were written. In a translation of this sonnet by Macgregor, the tercet is thus rendered:—

"'Tis well at least, breaking bad customs old,
    To change from eyes to feet—from these so wet
    By those if milder April should be met."

This is unintelligible; as indeed the original must have been to the translator, and also to the Abbé de Sade, who inserts this sonnet and his own version, and naively adds—" Je n'ai pas traduit les trois derniers vers de ce sonnet, parce que je n'y ai rien compris."

48. Many other similar cases might be adduced, in which the earnest student is indebted to the labours of the commentators; but I must now conclude with the remark, that should this attempt to place Petrarch on a higher level than he has yet attained through the medium of translations be at all encouraged, I have in view a second Work, to which this may serve as an introduction. Whether this Work succeed or fail, it will still supply me with pleasant memories of long winter evenings devoted to its composition. But I suppose a time

comes to most men, as it certainly has come to me, when they look with almost equal indifference both on failures and on successes. She who knew how to mitigate failures, and added pleasure to successes, reposes beneath the brow of Highgate Hill. The friends who cheered my fireside, accompanied me in my walks, or wrote pleasant letters, and discussed with me the various objects of our common pursuits and avocations, are nearly all gone. In losing them I have lost much of the stimulus to exertion that formerly gave elasticity to my work, and I am content to withdraw from the intellectual contest. I can, however, still enjoy a quiet kind of happiness in my books, while waiting for the time, now not far distant, when I too shall disappear. I feel like one who has gone a long way on a long journey, but homeward; with the knowledge that at my journey's end, she who has preceded me will be waiting for me with sweet smiles and loving welcome.

PART THE SECOND.

ILLUSTRATIONS FROM PETRARCH

OF

THE THREE TYPES AND THE VARIATIONS.

In the early editions of Petrarch the sonnets are not numbered, but are separated from each other by a blank space, as in the original codex in the Vatican Library. In the first numbered editions the same order is followed as in the earlier editions. After this, different Editors followed different systems, some giving a separate numbering to the sonnets in *La Morte*, to distinguish them from those in *La Vita;* others running the numbers through both parts, but including in a third part the sonnets that do not refer to Laura, and in a fourth the sonnets of doubtful authenticity. I have followed the numbering as given in the early editions, but in all cases quote the first line, or a portion thereof, so that the reader will find no difficulty in turning to any sonnet in the original if he consult the index of first lines, which usually accompanies every edition.

PART THE SECOND.

Type I.

1 2 2 1, 1 2 2 1,
3 4 5, 3 4 5.

Sonnet I.—*Voi, ch' ascoltate in rime sparse il suono.*

All ye who list in many a scattered rhyme,
    The sound of sighs with which my heart I fed,
    When my first youthful error me misled,
    Though now I'm somewhat changed by touch of time :
Long practising the Muse's varied chime,
    Now by vain hopes, now by vain sorrows led,
    If ever Love his influence on ye shed,
    A pardoning tear perchance your eyes may dim.
But now, full well I see how that my name,
    Has been too long a public jest, and I
    Have oft to bear of self-reproach the pain;
The fruit of all my folly is the shame
    Repentance brings; while I more clearly see
    That the world's joys are dreams, both brief and vain.

Tassoni has expended several pages of adverse criticism on this sonnet, most of it of the minute kind. For example, in the line that closes the first tercet—

Di me medesmo meco mi vergogno—

he objects to the *me me me mi;* while the very full line which closes the first quartet—

Quand' era in parte altr' uom da quel, ch' i 'sono,
(When I was partly a different man from what I am)—

he says is rather prose than poetry. Muratori, on the contrary, regards this as a fine line (O ye commentators!), and remarks that a poet cannot be always on the stilts, but must sometimes say what he has to say in language that might otherwise be prose. He commends this sonnet, although it does not contain any rare virtue, and thinks the poet need not be ashamed at having placed it in the vanguard of his poems. He points out the two lines that close the second quatrain as being happy, and even exquisite, but objects to the mode in which the tercets are connected with the quatrains; the word *Ma*, "but," not being well chosen. Moreover, the conclusion is not distinguished by much poetic fire.

Commentators disagree as to the sense in which the word *sparse*, "scattered," in the first line, is to be taken. Some are of opinion that it refers to the poems being scattered all over Italy; others to the fact that they are not continuous, like Dante's great poem, but are made up of small separate scattered poems.

SONNET XLVIII. } *Padre del Ciel, dopo i perduti*
TYPE I.   }   *giorni.*

Father of Heaven! forgive my misspent days,
  My nights, all passed in many a vain desire,
  Which wastes my heart in love's unholy fire,
  Thinking of charms, which, for my ill, I praise:
Vouchsafe to guide me into holier ways,
  To higher thoughts, that higher life inspire,
  So that my cruel enemy retire
  In rage, finding in vain, the snares he lays.
O Saviour mine! 'tis now th' eleventh year
  That I to this unholy yoke am tied
  (Who yield the most, feel most the weight and loss);

My grief, howe'er unworthy it appear,
O pity! deign my erring thought to guide
To this;—that Thou to-day wert on the cross.

This sonnet was written on a Good Friday, in remembrance of the Passion Week of 1327, in which Petrarch first saw Laura at the first hour of the 6th April. Muratori says that it is not a very high specimen of the poetic art, but that there is a grave, earnest tone about it that must commend itself to the reader. I may remark that the great simplicity and directness of the language render it difficult to do justice to this sonnet in an English translation. The specimens given in Bohn seem to me to be wanting in simplicity and directness, and they contain some positive errors. For example, the poet says in the first tercet that he has been eleven years under the yoke—

Che sopra i più soggetti è più feroce
Who yield the most, on them it hardest bears—

that is, those who most readily submit themselves to the yoke, on them it bears most cruelly. But the translator in Bohn has

" Relentless most to fealty most tried,"

which is not the idea.
The first line of the second tercet

Miserere del mio non degno affanno.
Pity my grief although it is unworthy.

This is rendered

" Pity my undeserved and lingering pains,"

which again misses the sense. The few simple words of the original
Com' oggi fosti in croce;
How this day Thou wast on the cross;

are thus amplified, and yet not translated—

" How on this day his cross, Thy Son, our Saviour bore."

SONNET LXXI. } *Piangete, donne, e con voi pianga*
TYPE I.   }   *Amore.*

Weep, ladies, weep! let Love your sorrow share!
   And weep, ye lovers too, of every clime!
   Since he is dead whose well-instructed rhyme
   Due reverence paid to you, while he lived here.
I pray that if I also add a tear,
   Our griefs commingled, may not harshly chime;
   Nor that my sighs be out of tune or time,
   Since to my anguished heart they bring some cheer.
Let many a rhyme and stanza tell our grief,
   For Cino, Master of the amorous strain,
   So lately taken from us, but too soon:
Pistoia's sons perverse! mourn ye in chief,
   That your sweet neighbour ye ne'er see again,
   While there is joy in heaven where he is gone.

Cino, or Guittoncino, was born in Pistoia in 1270, of the noble family of Sinibuldi. He was brought up to the study of the law, and in 1307 held the office of judge in his native city. He also lectured on jurisprudence, and there is a tradition that Petrarch was one of his pupils; but profited less from his lectures than from his hints in the art of making verses, and his instructive criticisms on his young pupil's rhymes. He is said to have introduced many reforms into the administration of the law, and by his verses and cultivation of literature to have had a powerful influence in promoting good taste. He was a personal friend of Dante, and exchanged verses with him. The lady of his love was named *Selvaggia*, which accounts for his frequent use of the adjective *selvaggio*. He died in 1336-7. A good edition of his works, by Ciampi, was published at Pisa in 1813, *Vita e Poesie di Messer Cino da Pistoia*.

Petrarch's sonnet "In Memoriam" flows placidly along, the thoughts, style, and versification being natural and limpid. The reference to the "perverse Pistoians," is an allusion to the banishment or voluntary expatriation of Cino during the contests of the civil factions. In one of his Canzoni he addresses Dante as a brother exile. The following is a translation of one of Cino's sonnets:—

CINO DA PISTOIA.

SONNET VII.
1 2 1 2, 1 2 1 2,
3 4 5, 3 4 5.
} *Sta nel piacer della mia Donna Amore.*

Love in my Lady's charms has fixed his seat,
   Like a star in heaven, or in the sun his rays,
   And on whose heart those eyes bright flashes beat,
   Grows spiritless; and captive her obeys.
His dazzled eyes dare not such splendour meet,
   Nor heart abide on which such beauty plays:
   But from his anguished breast must seek retreat:
   He tasks his skill, he who would sing her praise.
Her presence seems to clothe each place with smiles
   Where'er she goes; angelic is her gait;
   Noble her mien; humility her guide.
Her loving spirit soothes, consoles, beguiles;
   Discreet her speech; whence life and joy await
   On him who in her presence may abide.

SONNET CXI.
TYPE I.
} *Quand 'io v' odo parlar si dolcemente.*

When of thy voice I hear the melody,
   Which Love can aptly in his slaves inspire,
   My being kindles to a gentle fire,
   Such as might melt e'en Love's own enemy.
In every place my lady seems to be,
   Where sweetness and tranquillity retire,
   In beauty clad. Asleep, my sighs conspire,
   In place of other sounds, to waken me.
Her golden hair was streaming in the wind,
   Her head turned back to me: that image bright
   Has my heart's key, and knows the entrance well.

In my heart's treasure then such joy I find,
    That outward praise I have no power to write,
    Nor can my feeble tongue its splendours tell.

Sonnet CXII. Type I. } *Nè cosi bello il Sol giammai levarsi.*

The sun ne'er seemed to rise more bright or fair
    Upon a cloudless and transparent sky;
    Nor after rain, in many a varied dye
    The graceful bow celestial through the air,
Than to my ravished soul the vision rare,
    On that bright day when I began to sigh,
    Of that loved face; I use not praise too high,
    Saying, with her nought mortal can compare.
In those bright flashing glances Love appeared,
    With sovereign sweetness ruling: from that hour,
    All other objects seem to me obscure.
Sennuccio! seeing Love's bended bow upreared,
    I yearned to feel again that vision's power,
    And life to me has ceased to be secure.

Sonnet CXLIII. Type I. } *Per mezz' i boschi inospiti e selvaggi.*

Through a secluded forest, wild and drear,
    Where, e'en in arms, men risk a doubtful way,
    I pass secure; since nought can me dismay,
    Save the bright Sun of Love, that shines so clear.
Singing I go (my thoughts unwise but dear!)
    Of her, who still is nigh, where'er I stay;
    With dames and damsels there, I see her stray.
    But only pines and beeches see when near.

I seem to hear her when the zephyr sighs
   Through leaves, or birds complain, or water flows
   Amidst green grass whence rippling murmurs come:
The solitude that steeped in silence lies
   In this dark wood had lulled me to repose,
   But that my sun lost brightness through the gloom.

This sonnet was composed while the poet was travelling through the dangerous forest of Ardennes, as stated in the essay (§ 39, page 120, *ante*). Muratori considers it to be very little inferior to some of the best sonnets of the author. It begins well; and in the second quatrain the parenthetical exclamation (*O penser miei non saggi!*) is introduced with an unexpected grace. The thoughts are all beautiful, and especially that enamoured fantasy which sees its idol in every object around. The first tercet is charming, and the last line of the sonnet corrects the fantasy of the preceding lines.

Muzio suggests that *E vo cantando lei*, which opens the second quatrain, should be *cercando*, that is, "seeking her," not "singing her." Tassoni remarks that the poet was not seeking her who was already in his eye, and seemed to stand before him; and he contemptuously remarks that a man might just as well be seeking for the donkey on which he is riding. I give this piece of criticism not for its value, but as a specimen of the style sometimes adopted by the commentators. Other similar samples are to be found in the course of these notes.

It has been supposed that the last part of the first tercet may have been suggested by Virgil:—

   Et tenuis fugiens per gramina rivus.

SONNET CCX. } *Chi vuol veder quantunque può Natura.*
   TYPE I.

Who, heaven-taught Nature's highest work would find,
   Must hither come and gaze upon this one,
   Who shines, not to my eyes alone, a sun,
   But to the dull world, oft to virtue blind.

And quickly come, since Death oft leaves behind
    The bad, and garners 'mong the good alone :
    Such beauty lasts not !   Soon its course is run,
    For Heaven awaits it in its place assigned.
He will behold, should he arrive in time,
    All virtue, beauty, regal manners blent
    In one, with skill no art can emulate.
Then will he say that mute is all my rhyme,
    Such brilliant light beyond my genius went :
    He'll mourn his loss for aye, come he too late.

SONNET CCXLVII.   } *I' ho pien di sospir quest' aer*
    TYPE I.   *tutto.*

I've filled with sighs the circumambient air,
    Climbed the rude hills to view the lovely plain,
    Where she was born, who gave my young heart pain.
    And when mature, still held her conquest there.
She's gone to heaven, and left me to despair
    Her sudden flight; and I cannot restrain
    These eyes, grown weary seeking her in vain,
    From watering with my tears all objects here.
There's not a twig or stone among these hills,
    Nor verdant leaf or branch within these plains,
    Nor flower, nor blade of grass within these vales,
Nor drop of water from these founts distils,
    Nor beast that in these wild woods shelter gains,
    But knows how my sharp grief o'er me prevails.

Muratori's criticism on this sonnet seems to me to be just. He says that every word is well chosen, and every verse well filed (*ben limato*) ; but there is nothing remarkable about the idea, while the amplifications in the tercets would be easy to many a versifier vastly inferior to Petrarch.

Sonnet CCLX. } *Valle, che de 'lamenti miei se' piena.*
Type I.

O Valley ! echoing many a mournful lay,
   River ! that my sad tears so often swell,
   Ye sylvan beasts and birds ! ye too that dwell
In waters which 'tween flowery margins stray !
Ye winds ! that my warm sighs meet on their way,
   Sweet path ! that suits my mournful wanderings well,
   Hills once beloved ! that now of sorrow tell,
Where Love still calls ; and I, as wont, obey.
In all these objects well-known forms I see,
   While I, alas ! how changed ; my life once bright,
   Is now a source of painful, endless toil.
Here from this path, once trod by her and me,
   Her naked spirit took its heavenward flight,
   Its lovely tenement to earth a spoil.

This sonnet is one of the favourites with the commentators, but it is difficult to convey in a translation what Muratori characterises as the "grave, sweet, and affectionate tone" of the original. In spite of some exaggeration, the quartets give in few words a vivid idea of familiar natural objects, which the poet skilfully connects with himself in the first tercet. Nature remains the same, while we are often but too painfully conscious of change in ourselves, especially if we return to well-known scenes under the shadow of some great grief. The calm, majestic permanence of Nature appeals forcibly to us, especially as it seems remote from all human sympathy. It is a mark of power in the poet that, apparently with so little effort and in so few words, he can express so much

    Ben riconosco in voi l' usate forme,
    Non, lasso, in me ;

In the second tercet, Laura's spirit is described as going naked (*nuda*) to heaven, leaving on earth the beautiful form that clothed it (*la sua bella spoglia*). This is a bold figure, but I have endeavoured to follow my author as closely as possible.

SONNET CCLXI. } *Levommi il mio pensier in parte,*
TYPE I. } *ov' era.*

Raised by my thought, I found the region where
   She whom I seek, but here on earth in vain,
   Dwells among those who the third heaven gain,
And saw her lovelier and less haughty there.
She took my hand and said—" In this bright sphere,
   Unless my wish deceive, we meet again :
   Lo ! I am she who caused thee strife and pain,
And closed my day before the eve was near.
My bliss, no human thought can understand :
   I wait for thee alone—my fleshly veil
   So loved by thee is by the grave retained."
She ceased, ah why ? and why let loose my hand ?
   Such chaste and tender words could so prevail,
   A little more, I had in heaven remained.

I once asked a student of Shakspere which of his plays he preferred ? " The last I read !" was the reply. So, also, Petrarch's commentators are not agreed as to the best sonnet of their master. And it is a tribute to genius that there is no one play of Shakspere, any more than any one sonnet of Petrarch, that by universal consent is the best. Muratori, in his *Perfetta Poesia Italiana*, has taken great pains to show why he considers the sonnet before us as the best. In a later work he is content to class it as " one of the best, with few to equal it." It is marked by poetical invention : the ecstatic vision is vividly expressed, and there is a fulness, not only of sentiment but of detail, and a certain tenderness throughout, which cannot fail to awaken the sympathy of the attentive reader ; while the conclusion comes upon one with a sort of surprise. There is something irresistible in the idea that if

Laura had gone on talking a little longer his temporary visit to Heaven would have become a permanent residence.

The expression "less haughty" (*meno altera*) has received many comments; but there is no difficulty about it. While Laura was on earth she often repelled her lover's advances by a haughty bearing; which is now no longer needed. In the frequent ecstatic visions in which the poet sees her and talks with her, she is described as being manifold more lovely than when on earth; and although still humble, she is no longer proud or haughty.

> *Piena si d' umilta, vota d' orgoglio.*
> So full of humility, void of pride.

Some curious speculations have also been made on the expression *se 'l desir non erra* (which I have translated "unless my wish deceive"); for, it is asked, how could a beatified spirit have any doubt about the salvation of one still in the flesh? This is to confer prevision on the beatified spirit, and there is no reason to suppose that the faculties are so far enlarged as to include things that the Father "hath put in his own power." There are also curious speculations about the third heaven, "'l terzo cerchio," which was probably suggested to the poet by St. Paul (2 Cor. xxi. 2); but as these speculations, like the former, can lead to no conclusion, it is useless to pursue them.

To translate a sonnet that has been the object of so much admiration and comment thus becomes a formidable undertaking. But there is always this source of consolation in failure,—that I have endeavoured to follow the author as closely as possible, and have striven after that wonderful simplicity which in the hands of Petrarch becomes a real power. If I have not attained to it, the obvious reasons are that I am not an English Petrarch, and that our language is not the Italian.

SONNET CCLXII. } *Amor, che meco al buon tempo ti*
TYPE I.   }   *stavi.*

O Love! in happy times with me thou'dst go
    Along these banks, and thy old league with me
    We mused on, how it realised might be,
    Our thoughts still moving with the stream's soft flow;
Flowers, leaves, grass, waves, caves, airs that sweetly blow,
    Closed vales, high hills, and plains sunlit and free,
    My frequent refuge in my misery,
    From the rude strokes the tempests oft bestow.
Ye shadowy tenants of each verdant wood!
    Ye nymphs! and ye who feed and hide and play,
    In the clear crystal of the sedgy stream :
Ye know my days were passed in happy mood,
    Now darkened o'er by Death. No mortal may
    From the dread Sisters his own fate redeem.

Muratori remarks that the Graces must have assisted the poet in the composition of this sonnet, so charming is it : and he would place it among the best of the author, had the two concluding lines been more worthy of him. The first line of the second quatrain

Fior, fronde, erbe, ombre, antri, onde, aure soavi,

which has been praised for its overflowing fulness, will not move at all, according to Muratori, without the assistance of a windlass ; and the introduction of such harshness in the midst of so many sweet and pleasant objects he compares to the sound of a shrieking wheel in the midst of a concert of soft violins. It is not easy to read this line, omitting, as we must, the final vowels, although the poet has endeavoured to take off a little of the roughness by the introduction of *aure soavi* in which the final *e* is not cut off.

This is one of the sonnets of which the original draft is preserved, with corrections in the poet's handwriting.

The first quatrain is difficult to translate without the aid of the commentators.

> *Amor, che meco al buon tempo ti stavi*
> *Fra queste rive a' pensier nostri amiche;*
> *E per saldar le ragion nostre antiche,*
> *Meco, e col fiume ragionando andavi.*

Of course *al buon tempo* refers to the time when Laura was alive, and *saldar le ragioni* means "to settle accounts." According to Biagioli (and the other commentators agree with him), the argument is, that Petrarch had long and faithfully served Love, who had promised him the smiles of Laura, and this is the debt or account to be settled, and which they discussed while rambling on or near the banks of the Sorga. And since all surrounding objects knew of the poet's passion, they all, including the murmuring stream, plead with Love in his favour.

Unless all this be understood, the translator is in danger of converting this sonnet into an insipid pastoral. The following, from Bohn, is given as a translation of the first quatrain and the first line of the second, already quoted in the original:—

> "On these green banks in happier days I stray'd
> With Love, who whispered many a tender tale;
> And the glad waters, winding through the dale,
> Heard the sweet eloquence fond Love display'd.
> You, purpled plain, cool grot, and arching glade," etc.

If the reader has to form his opinion of Petrarch from such lines, it can no longer be a matter of surprise that he is thought tame and monotonous.

SONNET CCLXVIII.} *L' alto, e novo miracol, ch' a'*
TYPE I.   }   *di nostri.*

High miracle and rare! which, in our days,
  Shone in our world, but would not long remain.

  Which Heaven once showed us, Heaven took back
   again
  For the adornment of its starry ways.
 Love, who first loosed my tongue, would have me
   praise
  Her charms to those by whom she ne'er was seen ;
  To this work turned a thousand times in vain
  My mind, my time, pens, paper, ink, and lays.
 That to such height my rhymes not yet attain
  I know full well, and they too testify
  Who, worthily, to sound Love's praises, strive :
 Who know the truth, in silence will remain,
  Thinking that she surpassed all style, and sigh,
  " How blest the eyes that saw her when alive ! "

There is some difficulty as to the meaning of the first tercet, the opening line of which is

  Non son al sommo ancor giunte le rime,

literally

  The rhymes are not yet arrived at their height.

Biagioli supposes that the Poet meant to say that no poetry was sufficient to do justice to the charms of Laura. The other commentators, so far as I have consulted them, agree in supposing that the Poet refers to the Tuscan language as not being sufficient for the purpose, for it had not yet reached its greatest perfection, as he himself had proved, as well as all the poets of that period who wished to write worthily of love.

 I prefer to take the meaning as it lies on the surface, thinking that Biagioli's theory is supported by the second tercet. But there is much to be said in favour of the other view. Petrarch despised, or affected to despise, the vulgar tongue, esteeming Latin as the only language in which true poetry could be written. He never acquired a sufficient knowledge of Greek to read it critically, although he had a dim sense of the grandeur of Homer, for he says, " A man must be very strong to wrest from Hercules his club," referring to any one who dared to cope with Homer. And yet he had no ear for the grand and terrible and sweet music of Dante's great poem. [See APPENDIX.] One reason for this was that it was written in the vulgar tongue. Petrarch even professes to have been ashamed at that which really was his greatest honour, namely, having his own verses sung in the streets; and he regards "the hoarse applause of fullers, taverners, butchers, and other people of the like sort," as an insult to Dante's genius. Poor man! But perhaps we ought in justice to consider that before the invention of printing a man's works thus becoming popular were in danger of being corrupted, and of the corruptions thus engendered finding their way into future hand-written copies; so that the very popularity of the poet might prove an injury to his fame. It must also be remembered that the term " polite," as applied to literature, was something more than a name. Letters were intended only for the polite; and it was not until printing had greatly multiplied books that the area of polite literature assumed sufficient proportions to include all classes.

That the Italian language made great progress under the Troubadours, is evident from their numerous poems already referred to [ESSAY, § 11]; and following up their method, succeeding poets sang the charms of their respective ladies in poetry which gradually improved in grace and power. Thus Dante had his Beatrice, Cino his Selvaggia, Guido Cavalcanti his Mandetta, Petrarch his Laura, Boccaccio his Fiammetta, Montemagno his Lauretta, and so on. It may therefore be fairly asked if the language was not yet sufficiently matured in the verses of the above-named poets, what hope was there of its ever arriving at perfection?

That Petrarch himself became aware of the importance of the literature to which he had so largely contributed, is evident from the facts already stated [ESSAY, § 25, 26]; and in a letter to Boccaccio, written in his sixty-second year, he says—" I wished to devote myself entirely to poetry in the vulgar tongue, for since it has of late been cultivated and polished, it appears to me to be susceptible of new develop-

M

ments; whereas Latin prose and verse have attained such perfection that nothing can be added to them. Following up this idea, I collected materials for an important work; but looking at the age, so full of pride and ignorance, and seeing that I lost my time, and that my verses were mangled by the people, I abandoned the project." Petrarch was probably thinking of his own poems when he wrote " of late," in the above passage.

SONNET CCLXXXIII. } *L' aura, e l' odore, etc.*
TYPE I.

The air, the odour, and the cooling shade
    Of the sweet laurel, and its sight in bloom,
    Repose and brightness of my life of gloom,
    Death took away, who maketh all things fade.
As when the Sun by his Sister dark is made,
    So my high light is quenched in the like doom;
    I pray that aid 'gainst Death from Death may come;
    To such dark thoughts by Love am I betrayed!
O beauteous Lady! thou hast slept brief sleep,
    And waking, found thyself 'mong spirits blest;
    Where souls their home with the soul's Maker find:
And if my rhymes have any power to keep
    Thee dear among the noblest minds and best,
    On Time's high forehead they thy name will bind.

Muratori points out a little confusion of thought in the figure of the laurel tree. We may enjoy its odour and its shade, but it does not give us air or coolness. Instead of rendering literally the line—*L' aura, e l' odore, e 'l refrigerio, e l' ombra*, I have combined the last two nouns into "cooling shade," which gets rid of part of the objection. The old play upon the words of *L' aura* the air, *laura* the laurel, and *Laura* the lady, is kept up in the first quatrain, and lies partly concealed in the second tercet. Of course the line

    Come a noi 'l Sol, se sua soror l' adombra,

literally " as when with us the sun is made dark by his sister" (that is, the moon), refers to an eclipse of the sun.

Muratori directs attention to the splendid line

> *Io cheggio a Morte incontr 'a Morte aita;*

So that I pray to Death 'gainst Death for aid ;

and also points out the first tercet as being marked by "a sweet, admirable, and exquisite image, due as much to fancy as to reflection : "

> *Dormito hai, bella Donna, un breve sonno :*
> *Or se' svegliata fra gli spirti eletti,*
> *Ove nel suo Fattor l' alma s' interna.*

We suppose that when alive we are awake, and when dead, asleep. Our poet in a striking and elegant manner shows us the contrary. He also terminates the sonnet with a noble tercet, which, however, reminds us of Virgil :—

> Si quid mea carmina possunt
> Nulla dies umquam memori vos eximet aevo.

SONNET CCLXXXIX.
TYPE I.
} *Vide fra mille Donne una già tale.*

'Mong many Ladies one had so much grace,
  And so assailed my heart with amorous fear,
  That to my ardent fancy it was clear,
  She must belong to the celestial race.
Nothing in her of mortal could I trace,
  She seemed to breathe a heavenly atmosphere :
  My soul now warmed by hope, now chilled by fear,
  Essayed its wings in vain to reach her place.
Too high she soared for my terrestrial weight,
  And soon, alas ! she vanished from my sight ;
  The thought still makes me torpid with alarm.

O sweet and lucid eyes! that formed the gate
  By which that power, whose terrors so affright,
  Found means of entrance to so fair a form.

In the second tercet the poet gives expression to the opinion that in dying, the eyes are the first to feel the hand of death.

SONNET CCXCI. } *Questo nostro caduco, e fragil bene.*
  TYPE I.

This fragile good, as fleeting as the air,
  Or passing shadow, which we beauty name,
  Was never seen, 'till in this age it came,
  In one concentred—source of my despair.
Nature wills not, nor is it fitting her,
  To make one rich, all others poor proclaim;
  To heap her gifts on one her only aim—
  (Pardon, ye fair! or ye who think ye're fair).
Such beauty ne'er on earth was seen before,
  Nor, I believe, will be: 'twas so concealed,
  The world scarce knew the treasure it contained:
Soon lost! but I th' exchange cease to deplore;
  How bright those charms heaven here to me revealed,
  Beatified, they manifold transcend.

Tassoni remarks that the second tercet of this sonnet is not a nut for every tooth [*Questo ternario non è nocciuola per ogni dente*]. Castelvetro suggests that by *poca vista* the poet refers to the decay of his sight as he became old—

  onde 'l cangiar mi giova
  La poca vista a me dal Cielo offerta,
  Sol per piacer alle sue luci sante.

Tassoni supposes that reference is made to the exaltation of Laura's charms in heaven, as if the poet had said—" But I rejoice to change for the limited view of her that heaven granted me here, a sight of her more perfect beauty above."

This theory seems to be borne out by reference to sonnet ccxcv., *Cenobbi, quanto il Ciel*, etc. (a translation of which is given at p. 173); in which the poet, in the first quatrain, appreciates Laura's earthly charms so far as heaven had opened his eyes; but that in her beatified state she was surrounded by so many wonders that his feeble sight was not able to gaze upon them, still less to describe them. This by no means implies defective sight; for in the charming figure with which this sonnet is concluded, he says [I give it in the form of a couplet]—

> For he who on the sun has fixed his sight,
> Less clearly sees, the brighter is the light.

SONNET CCCIII. } *Donna, che lieta col principio nostro.*
TYPE I.

Lady! thou 'rt happy with thy Maker now,
    Since thy pure life has earned its guerdon meet,
    Raised to that glorious and lofty seat,
    In richer sheen than pearls and gold bestow;
'Mong other Ladies high and rare art thou:
    In sight of Him who seeth all, repeat
    The story of my love, faith pure and sweet,
    Which caused my tears and all my rhymes to flow.
Thou know'st my heart on earth was always thine,
    As now it is in heaven; nor ever turned,
    But to regard the sunshine of thine eyes;
Hence to repay the strife that long was mine,
    In seeking thee, when all things else I spurned,
    I pray that to thy presence soon I rise.

SONNET CCCVI. } *L' aura mia sacra al mio stanco*
TYPE I.   *riposo.*

Her sacred spirit in my weariness
    Of sleep, breathes o'er me oft; I courage take

Say what I've suffered, suffer, for her sake,
  Which, while she lived, I never dared confess.
I tell her of that look of tenderness,
  Which bade my long tormenting passion wake;
  How Love a varying sport of me would make,
  One hour in bliss, the next in wretchedness.
In silent pity she my story hears,
  Still gazing on me, and in sympathy,
  She sighs meanwhile, and then begins to weep.
My soul, o'ercome with sadness at her tears,
  And vexed at having caused them, back to me
  Weeping returns, and I wake up from sleep.

SONNET CLXXIII. } *Rapido fiume, che d' alpestra*
  TYPE II.   }   *vena.*

TO THE RHODANUS (the Rhone).

O rapid river! from the Alpine side,
  Eroding on, thou and thy name agree;
  Restless descending, night and day, with me,
  I led by Love; Nature alone thy guide.
Go on before! sleep never bids thee bide,
  Nor weariness; but ere thou reach the sea,
  Stay where thy banks more verdant seem to be,
  And where the zephyrs more serenely glide.
My own sweet living Sun thou there wilt meet,
  That gives to thy left bank its grace and bloom:
  Ah! dare I hope my absence makes her greet!
Let kisses say instead of words, "He'll come!"
  Kiss thou her beautiful white hands, her feet;
  My mind goes with thee; toils my strength consume.

This sonnet was written while the poet was travelling along the Rhone to Avignon, the Italian name *Rodano* being derived apparently from *rodere*, "to erode;" but some suppose its name is from *Roda*, a place near its source.

The poet Thomas Moore seems to have derived from this sonnet the idea of his charming song :—

> "Flow on, thou shining river,
> But ere thou reach the sea."

In fact, this second line may be taken as a translation of Petrarch's

> *e pria che rendi*
> *Suo dritto al mar.*

The poet, weary with his journey, bids the river flow on and seek Laura with a message—

> "Seek Ella's bower, and give her," etc.

Muratori speaks of the evident amenity of this sonnet taking its place among the best of the author. He thinks it a charming idea to treat the river as an intelligent being, and to make it a gentle ambassador to Laura, to whose influence he attributes the more flowery aspect and the serener air of its left bank ; but he objects to the closing line, which is a quotation of the sacred words " the spirit is willing, but the flesh is weak," being introduced into a love sonnet ; and in deference to this objection I have given different words, while retaining the sense.

It may be hypercritical to object to the last line of the first quatrain,

> *Ov' Amor me, te sol Natura mena,*

on the ground that nature displays herself in love, as in the descent of a river. The poet may have intended by the introduction of the word *sola*, "alone," to imply that the offices of love involve far more complicated efforts and details than are concerned in the simple descent of a river : but the more probable supposition is that in the time of Petrarch man was not regarded as a part of nature, but as an exalted being, or one capable of exaltation, and standing out distinctly from surrounding phenomena.

I have introduced into the first tercet the Scotch word

"greet," to "shed tears," or "to weep;" and into the first quatrain a technical but expressive word, derived from the *erosion* of the geologists. Dryden objects to the introduction of technical terms into poetry, such as those " of navigation, land-service, or the cant of any profession," on the ground that Virgil avoided them " because he writ not for mariners, soldiers, astronomers, gardeners, peasants, etc., but to all in general, and, in particular, to men and ladies of the first quality, who have been better bred than to be more nicely knowing in the terms. In such cases 'tis enough for a poet to write so plainly that he may be understood by his readers to avoid impropriety, and not affect to be thought learned in all things."

In modern practice, and under the altered conditions of education, the moderate use of technical terms in poetry seems to be an advantage; since they are the shortest and most expressive exponents of thought, while the effort to avoid them often leads to loose and inaccurate statements. Of course it is not always easy to say that a given word is a purely technical one—that is, limited to the art or science which employs it. But the tendency of advancing knowledge is to take words out of their technical meshes, and set them free into the broad stream of general language. In this way words may be classed into purely technical words, and words in common use that have also a technical application. Many words that were invented to supply the wants of art and science, and were properly technical in their origin and early use, were found so convenient and expressive, that they gradually became incorporated into the common stock of words, and found their place in an ordinary, as distinguished from a technological, dictionary. If we suppose the measure of technical words to have been full in Dryden's time, it would probably have become nearly empty long before this, were it not that advancing knowledge continued the supply. How long a word remains technical depends on circumstances, among which we may not reckon the over-education of " men and ladies of the first quality," for the tendency at the present time is rather to strive after technical knowledge than to be supposed to be ignorant of it. And I suppose Dryden would not object to the use of an expressive word although it had not yet fairly escaped from its technical entanglement. Indeed, the circumstance of his using it would tend to set it free. But he would justly object to the use of such nautical terms as Falconer has introduced into his "Shipwreck," some of which are intelligible only to the sailor. The rule, then, seems to be this,—That purely technical words are not to be used, but technical words that have more or less escaped into the language may be employed.

SONNET CCV. } *Fresco, ombroso, fiorito, e verde colle.*
TYPE II.

O flower-enamelled hill! fresh, shady, green,
   Where musing now, now bent on minstrelsy,
   An angel seated there she seems to be,
   And beauty fades before her, beauty's queen.
Throned in my heart, as she so long has been,
   I would not have my heart return to me,
   But make it follow her fair feet, to see
   Them bless the flowers—my tears their dewy sheen.
At every step my heart's sad throes complain;
   "Let pity for him move thy gentle will,
   With tears he's weary, weary with life's pain."
Fair hill, she smiles! unequal parts we fill;
   Thou'rt paradise—I heartless rock remain—
   O sacred, fortunate and happy hill!

SONNET CCXLVI. } *Sennuccio mio, benche doglioso,*
TYPE II.   *e solo.*

SENNUCCIO—IN MEMORIAM.

O my Sennuccio! though sad and lone
   Thou'st left me, consolation yet I find,
   Since from th' embodied sepulchre of mind
   Thou'rt free, and heavenward on glad pinions flown;

Thy sight enlarged, takes in each pole and zone,
   What powers the stars, in devious orbits bind;
   Thou seest how much our vision is confined;
   Thy bliss allays the losses I bemoan.
But much I pray, do thou in that third sphere,
   Greet Cino, Dante, and Guittone well,
   Our Franceschin, that band of friends all dear:
And that I live in tears, my Lady tell;
   Her charms remembering, and her goodness here,
   Like some wild beast in solitude I dwell.

This sonnet was composed in 1349, when the plague, raging throughout Italy, had already carried off many of Petrarch's best friends; the land was also torn by earthquakes; and war and strife filled the land. The calamities were so great that, as Petrarch remarks in one of his letters, "posterity, if there be one, will not give credit to our narratives." Sennuccio Delbene is described by the poet as being one of his oldest and wisest friends (*antico e saggio*). It is supposed that it was in his garden that Petrarch met Laura on May-day 1347, when the old man gathered two of his best roses, and presented one to each of his visitors, with the remark that he had never seen such lovers. This incident is described in the 207th Sonnet, *Due rose fresche*, etc.

The sonnet on the death of Sennuccio is somewhat meagre in style, and does not partake of the rich vein of thought that produced the best sonnets of our author. The last line seems to have been suggested by the remark of Aristotle (whose works Petrarch knew through the medium of a Latin translation), that they who live in solitude, apart from their fellows, ought either to be beasts or more than men. In the first tercet the collocation of Dante's name with the names of inferior poets has led to the remark that Petrarch was jealous of Dante. On this point some details are given in the Appendix, No. vi. I may also refer to the annotation on Sonnet cclxviii. (page 161, *ante*). In the sonnet now before us, the names mentioned are those of sonnet-writers, personal friends of Dante. Fra Guittone has the merit of having established the regular sonnet in Italy. He was not a monk, but a brother of a military order. The following is a translation of one of his sonnets. A specimen of Cino's muse has been already given at page 151, *ante*.

Fra Guittone.

Type I.—*Quanto piu mi distrugge il mio pensiero.*

The more my thought dissolves in constant moan,
    The more her cruelty produces pain,
    The more I sink in thoughts, alas! how vain;
    And with the flight of hope, I still hope on.
And reasoning with myself, the truth must own,
    That I must sink beneath the load is plain;
    Yet I, my strong desire, cannot restrain,
    From loving, seeking what my bane has grown.
But it may chance that after many a year,
    Reading the rhymes that echo all my sighs,
    Some one may sympathise with my hard fate.
Who knows but she, to whom I'm now not dear,
    My loss, as causing hers, may recognise,
    And mourn my death in accents passionate!

Sonnet CCLXIV. } *Anima bella, da quel nodo sciolta.*
   Type II.

O beauteous soul! set free from thy earth's tie,
    That masterpiece of Nature's loveliness,
    O deign from heaven my life obscure to bless,
    Once glad, now marked by many a tearful sigh.
The false opinion which, while I was nigh,
    Made thy sweet face cold, harsh disdain express,
    Has left thy heart; and now 'twere happiness,
    Would'st thou look down and to my sighs reply.
See the huge rock from which the Sorga springs,
    And see me lonely by its margin green,
    My food the sorrow that thy memory brings:

Let not thy dwelling, nor aught else be seen,
  That vexes thee among these rural things,
  Scene of thy birth, of our love's birth the scene.

This sonnet is one among many proofs to be found in Petrarch's works, in opposition to the Abbé de Sade's theory, namely—1. That Laura was not born at Avignon, but rather in a small rural district in its neighbourhood ; 2. That she was never married ; 3. That when Petrarch fell in love with her she was only twelve or thirteen years of age, and not about twenty and two years a wife ; 4. That when the poet refers to his falling in love, he describes it as happening in the country, and not in the Church of S. Chiara at Avignon ; 5. That she died and was buried at Cabrieres, near Vaucluse, and not at Avignon. These points are briefly discussed in a Note in the APPENDIX.

SONNET CCLXIX. } *Zefiro torna, e 'l bel tempo*
  TYPE II.   *rimena.*

Zephyr returns, and the sweet season brings,
  With flowers and grass, all Flora's crew to hail ;
  The swallow warbles, mourns the nightingale,
  And spring expands her variegated wings.
Serene the sky ; for joy each meadow sings ;
  Jove gladly sees his daughter's might prevail ;
  Air, waters, earth, repeat the amorous tale,
  And love reanimates all living things.
But woe is me ! by many a sigh opprest,
  Drawn from my heart by her who took its key,
  When she departed to the region blest ;
All seems a desert of wild beasts to me,
  The song of birds, the meads in beauty drest,
  E'en lovely woman's honest courtesy.

SONNET CCLXXIX. } *Sento l' aura mia antica, e i*
TYPE II.   }   *dolci colli.*

I feel the well-known breeze, and, yonder see
   The hills beloved, the source of that sweet light
   Which, as heaven willed, was now my eyes' delight,
   And now the cause of tears and misery.
Ye foolish thoughts! and hopes delusive ye!
   Widowed the trees; turbid the streams unite;
   Empty and cold the nest she made so bright,
   Where still I live, but rather dead would be,
Hoping for respite, that I might retire
   From my soft plaints, and so much anxious pain,
   From the bright eyes that set my heart a-fire.
But him I serve still cruel must remain:
   He made me burn while lived my soul's desire,
   Now o'er her scattered dust to weep in vain.

The poet, returning from Padua to Vaucluse, in approaching Cabrieres began to feel the air that Laura breathed, and to see the sweet hills that had become widowed by her death. He complains that Love is still cruel and exacting, since he tormented him during Laura's life, and still continues to do so after her death. This is one of the few examples in which the second quatrain is run into the first tercet.

SONNET CCXCV. } *Conobbi, quanto il Ciel gli occhi*
TYPE II.   }   *m'aperse.*

I knew, so far as Heaven had cleared my sight,
   And Love and Study had upborne my wings,
   Things new and beautiful, but mortal things,
   Which every star shed on one object bright.
But my dull vision cannot bear the light
   Of strange vague forms some force celestial brings,

Immortal, high as their eternal springs,
  Nor my dull intellect conceive their might.
So that, whate'er I sing of her in praise,
  Who, for my praises, prays to God for me,
  Seems but a drop from the abyss to raise:
No song above the singer's mind can be:
  And he who on the sun hath fixed his gaze,
  More bright the light, less clearly can he see.

Tassoni ranks this not only as the finest of Petrarch's sonnets, but as one that has not been equalled by any other poet. Muratori thinks Tassoni might have been content with naming it the most magnificent of our poet, without placing it above the sonnets of other writers. Nevertheless, he admits it to be a rare and noble production. The verses run with nerve and vigour; the periods are conducted with majesty; the epithets are luminous, and the whole matter weighty.

But when the commentators reduce this poem to plain prose I cannot agree with their interpretation. They suppose that in the first quatrain the poet refers to the beauties of Laura's person, and in the second to those of her mind. Ought we not rather to say that the first quatrain refers to Laura in her earthly state, and the second to her beatified state? He could to a certain extent understand and describe the first, but was quite unequal to a description of the second. He had but a dim vision of her spiritual state, surrounded as it was by heavenly beings, so strange and unusual and splendid, that his intellect was not able to understand them or his vision to face their brilliancy. The tercets seem to carry out this idea, and their beauty and originality render them worthy companions of the noble quatrains.

In rendering this sonnet into English I admit the difficulty of the task and the feebleness of the execution; but as I have endeavoured to keep as close as possible to the original, the reader, it is hoped, will gain from it some idea of the beauty of this striking production.

SONNET CCXCIX. } *Ripensando a quel, ch'oggi il Cielo*
  TYPE II.   }   *onora.*

Who heaven adorns, each thought brings back again;
  That look, when she her golden head inclined;
  That face; the angelic modest voice that twined
  My heart with sweetness,—fills it now with pain.
I marvel how I've lived, and life were vain,
  But, ere the dawn, to tranquillise my mind,
  Her pure and lovely presence here I find;
  More pure than lovely, must in doubt remain.
How of those chaste and pious meetings tell!
  When, all intent on sympathy, she hears
  What woes the history of my love befel.
When to her sense, the morning's light appears,
  She flies to heaven,—the way she knows so well,
  Her eyes are full, each cheek is wet with tears.

SONNET CCCII. } *Gli Angeli eletti, e l' anime beate.*
  TYPE II.   }

The elect of Angels, and the Spirits blest,
  The denizens of heaven, on the first day
  My Lady went to swell that bright array,
  Surrounded her with wondering, pious quest.
" What light is this? who this new beauteous guest?
  Such loveliness," among themselves they say,
" From yonder erring world ne'er found the way,
  In all this age, to this our realm of rest."
She happy, thus, her changed abode to find,
  Takes equal rank with the most perfect there;
  But now and then she casts a look behind,

To see if I should follow: such her care.
    Hence, all my thoughts are heavenward now inclined,
    Knowing, that soon I join her, is her prayer.

SONNET XXV. } *Quanto più m' avvicino al giorno estremo.*
TYPE III.

The nearer I approach to life's last day,
    Which only can cut short our mortal woe,
    More swiftly seems the stream of life to flow,
    And hopes, from time, prove false and pass away.
And to my thoughts, "Not long can last," I say,
    "Our love-song, since this earthly load will go,
    Though hard and heavy, melting like fresh snow,
    And we thenceforth shall gain a peaceful way."
For with that load, the hopes take wings and fly,
    That fed so long the passion in my breast,
    With smiles and tears, with anger and with fear;
And clearer see how men are oft distrest,
    And how too often they but vainly sigh
    For ills which, to their fancy, but appear.

Tassoni says that this sonnet is *molto ben tirato*, "very well drawn out." Muratori does not regard it as a *capo d'opera*, or "first-rate work," although it makes good harmony.

Two translations of this sonnet are given in Bohn's collection. In the first, by Wrangham, the opening lines,

> *Quanto più m' avvicino al giorno estremo,*
> *Che l' umana miseria suol far breve;*

are thus translated,—

> "Near and more near as life's last period draws,
>   Which oft is hurried on by human woe."

This is both awkward and inaccurate. The idea is not that

human woe hurries on death, but that death alone is able to arrest human woe.

This translator also makes a curious mistake in the second tercet,—

Si vedrem chiaro poi come sovente
Per le cose dubbiose altri s' avanza,
E come spesso indarno si sospira.

"Then shall we clearly trace why *some are blest*,
Through deepest misery raised to Fortune's top,
And why so many sighs so oft are heaved in vain."

There is not a word in the original of the passage underlined. The fact is, the translator was caught in the trap set by the verb *s' avanza*, which, there could be no doubt, must mean "advances himself." Now, according to the dictionary of Villanuova, *avanzarsi* is used figuratively "to express progress in good or in ill, in persons as well as things," so that the poet really says that "often one advances himself in ill for doubtful things." The commentators take the same view, and interpret *s' avanza* by *s' affanna*, "vexes himself," for by doing so a person may be said to advance in ill.

SONNET LXIX. } *Erano i capei d' oro a l'aura sparsi.*
TYPE III.

Her golden hair was streaming in the wind,
  Which sweetly twisted it a thousand ways;
  And in those eyes' unutterable gaze
Flashed a bright light, which now is dimmed, I find.
Her face, for me, expressed a loving mind,
  (Did truth or self-deceit that fancy raise?)
  What marvel that my heart was soon ablaze,
Love finding food for fire, to Love consigned!
Her walk was not the step of mortal thing,
  But of angelic form; her accents clear
  Had in their music more than human sound:
A heavenly spirit did I see and hear,
  A living sun; and if such charms take wing,
  The slackening of the bow heals not the wound.

The fault-finding Tassoni places this sonnet among the very best of his author; characterised, as it is, by ease and sweetness, and a sort of undefined stateliness, which forms the perfection of a graceful style; while objects which otherwise appear common, here become rare by the mode of handling. The more judicious Muratori is equally enthusiastic;—he styles it *bello bellissimo;* and Biagioli calls it *divino.* According to Muratori this sonnet breathes a sort of unusual poetic fervour, which takes hold of the reader, from the simple and clear introduction to the final termination; and he fancies the poet must have had other words in his mind; but the image of Laura, as she first appeared to him, overcame them, and took the first place. The poetic fervour rises in the tercets, which contain many admirable exaggerations, well adapted to a lover and a poet in a nearly incandescent state. Every line has a spirited movement about it; the sentiments are clearly and beautifully expressed, and the rhymes arise naturally. In short, the poet's Pegasus takes some graceful bounds from the quatrains to the first tercet, and from this to the second. The ingenious figure which closes the second quatrain is introduced by an easy illation; but this figure, however elegant and poetical it may appear to the Italian, contains something of the risible to an English mind. I have endeavoured in the above translation to express the meaning in another way.

> *I', ché l' esca amorosa al petto avea,*
> *Qual maraviglia, se di subit 'arsi?*
>
> I, who had amorous tinder at my breast,
> What marvel if it suddenly took fire?

Petrarch's sonnets had made the beauty of Laura so famous, that travellers were curious to see her. It is said that one such, who saw her in her decline, expressed his surprise that such beauty should have inspired such ardent poetry; and that this remark being reported to the poet, led to the composition of this sonnet. Its leading idea refers to his first meeting with Laura, when she was in the full glow of youth and beauty, the wind spreading out her hair; but now, many years after, although her charms are dimmed, the poet's love remains the same. He briefly describes her hair, the marvellous beauty of her eyes, and to his fancy the kind expression of her face. What marvel then if he fell in love at first sight?

The sonnet winds up with a charming figure, not the less so because it comes unexpectedly, with a sort of surprise, and requires a little reflection before we feel its beauty and propriety. Laura's charms, which moved the poet's love, have suffered either through age or sickness, but the love remains the same. The arrow having inflicted its wound, the unstringing of the bow cannot cure it.

With reference to the first tercet the reader may be reminded of Virgil:—

> Et vera incessu patuit Dea;
> Nec vox hominem sonat.

SONNET LXXX. } *Lasso! ben so che dolorose prede.*
TYPE III.

Alas! too well I know what dolorous prey
    Death makes of us, who no one deigns to spare,
    That men indifferent grow to what was dear,
    And in short time their promises gainsay:
I see much suffering no ruth repay,
    And in my heart the last day's knell I hear;
    Love still exacts his tribute, many a tear,
    Yet from my prison will not ope the way.
So as I mark how moments, hours, and days
    Steal years, I do not to deception bend,
    But to a higher power than magic spell.
Passion and reason twice seven years contend,
    The worthier yet will victory gain and praise,
    If mortal mind can its own good foretell.

Tassoni has an odd remark on this sonnet, namely, that he must be stolid who does not praise this one, and equally so who praises them all. Muratori terms it a vigorous sonnet, full of grave matter, handled with considerable poetic skill; but he prefers the quatrains to the tercets.

In this sonnet, the poet, knowing the instability of human things, takes shame to himself for still following Love, who attracts him with a force stronger than that of magic art, the business of which is to deceive, whereas Love is a real power to which he has so long submitted. The poet seems to have had in his mind the expression of St. Paul: "What I would, that I do not; but what I hate, that do I" (Rom. vii. 15). He is still contending with his passion, but hopes to secure the conquest of mind over matter.

SONNET CCXLVIII. } *L' alma mia fiamma oltra le belle*
TYPE III.   }   *bella.*

Love-feeding flame! beauty herself excelling,
  On which kind Heaven bestowed its favour high,
  Is quenched too soon for me, and, in the sky,
  Has late regained yon star, her native dwelling.
I now begin to wake; see her repelling
  My young desire, and, for my good, each sigh;
  I now can read the eloquent reply
  Her look conveyed, of sweetness, coldness telling.
I thank her now for counsel high and wise,
  That with a lovely face and sweet disdain,
  Turned burning thoughts to thoughts of purity.
Ah gentle Artifice, good ends to gain!
  I with my song, she with her teaching eyes,
  To her gave glory, virtue gave to me.

This is one of the best of Petrarch's sonnets. Why it is so, Muratori in his youthful days was not able to say, because, being, in common with the work of all good poets, a strong and manly composition, it requires judgment for its due appreciation, and that is the very quality young men lack;— they rather prefer poetry that is interwoven with flowery conceits. The sonnet opens with a lovely symphony, the elevated style of which is maintained throughout; the thoughts are poetical and exact, the rhymes well chosen, and not a word that can be spared. It is like one of Raffaelle's pictures, which improves in beauty the more the object of the artist is understood. How far the translation responds to this criticism must be left to the accomplished Italian scholar. If he approve, no one else has the right to condemn.

SONNET CCCVII. }
TYPE III. } *Ogni giorno mi par più di mill 'anni.*

More than a thousand years appears each day
   In following her, my faithful leader dear,
   My guide in this world, now my pioneer
   To happier life, by a more perfect way.
Nor can the world's allurements bid me stay;
   For in my heart a heaven-born light shines clear,
   That makes the world at its true worth appear,
   And I begin my losses to assay.
Nor need I fear what death reserves in store,
   Since He, my Saviour, felt that pain supreme,
   That I might boldly meet the final hour;
And she, who of my verse inspired the theme,
   Has lately felt in every vein his power,
   And slept in death as in a pleasant dream.

One of the commentators remarks that if Laura guided the poet in this world, it must have been by the path of virtue. By what better path (*miglior via*) could she have conducted him to a happier life (*vita senza affanni*)? Surely such a comment is superfluous, since in the first tercet the poet expresses his *faith* in HIM, the King, who suffered death in its acutest form.

Che 'l Re sofferse con più grave pena.

We also open our eyes with wonder when another commentator thinks "the King" (*il Re*) ambiguous, since it may refer to the King of France or to the King of Spain, the subjects of each of whom claim precedence for their own sovereign. Such commentary as this is childish, especially as the poet expressly says that the example of that death no longer makes him fear death.

The first line of this sonnet,

Ogni giorno mi par più di mill' anni,

has been claimed for the Provençal poet Luigi Americi; but it seems to have been hardly worth taking from him, or contesting when claimed.

First Variation of the Quatrains.

1 2, 1 2, 1 2, 1 2,
3 4 5, 4 3 5. } Tercets as in Type III.

SONNET LIX.—*S' al principio risponde il fine e' l mezzo.*

If of the fourteenth year of my long woe,
    Middle and end like the beginning be,
    In vain I seek cool shade, in vain I go
        To meet the breeze, Love's flame so grows in me.
No means to rule my thoughts will Love bestow
    For 'neath his yoke, not e'en my breath is free:
    And she hath caused me half away to flow
        Through eyes still turned upon her constantly.
Thus wasting go I on from day to day
    In secret grief, which I alone know well,
    And she whose glances melt my softened heart:
How life endured till now, I scarce can tell,
    Nor know how long with me will be its stay
    Since death draws near, life hastens to depart.

This sonnet is one of inferior workmanship, and would not be introduced here but as an illustration of the peculiar metrical arrangement of which it is the only specimen. It may be taken as an illustration of the remark in the Essay (15) that the more widely the poet departs from the regular types the less happy is the expression of his muse. In the original there is an awkward use of the word *mezzo*, which closes the first, fifth, and seventh lines of the quatrains : in the first use the word means "the middle ;" in the second, "bounds ;" and in the third, "quantity."

First Variation of the Quatrains.

1 2, 1 2, 1 2, 1 2, } Tercets as in Type II.
3 4 3, 4 3 4.

Sonnet CCXL.—*Quante fiate al mio dolce ricetto.*

How oft I wander to my loved retreat,
   Others, and if I can, myself to fly,
   My breast, the herbage round, with tears I greet,
   And agitate the air with many a sigh.
How oft I wander, and my griefs repeat,
   In the dark woods, that shut out all the sky ;
   Seeking, in thought, my soul's delight to meet,
   Whom Death has ta'en ; for Death's release call I.
I call on her from Sorga's waters clear,
   To rise as nymph, or goddess of the flood,
   And on the bank before me reappear.
Ah yes ! on the fresh grass but now she stood
   Among the flowers ; her very self was there,
   Her look in sympathy with my sad mood.

Muratori remarks that although this sonnet cannot take rank among Petrarch's highest flights, it contains so many beauties as to entitle it to an honourable post. The diction is good, the thought is full and well elaborated in the quatrains, while the imagination has full play in the tercets. The love of solitude is impressively given in the second line,—

Fuggendo altrui, e, s' esser può me stesso.

His grief on the death of Laura is well expressed in the succeeding lines, as also his own desire to follow her. In a graceful manner he brings Laura into the solitary place, and represents her so vividly that the reader fancies he can see her as well as the poet.

Second Variation of the Quatrains.

1 2, 1 2, 2 1, 2 1,
3 4 3, 4 3 4. } Tercets as in Type II.

Sonnet CCXXXVIII.—*Se lamentar augelli, o verdi fronde.*

What time birds pipe their plaint, and every tree
   Its green arms rustles in the summer air,
   And on the fresh and flowery banks, to me
   Comes the hoarse murmur of the waters clear;
Pensive, I write of Love, while seated here;
   And her whom Heaven once showed, earth-hid, I
     see;
   I feel her living yet; though distant, near,
   And answering all my sighs in sympathy.
I hear her pitying words—" Why thus in woe,
   So prematurely waste thy life, and why
   Cause from those eyes that piteous stream to flow?
Weep not for me—I dying, did not die;
   I only seemed to close my eyes, for know
   I opened them in heaven's own light on high."

The above sonnet, which is the only example of this metrical variation, is placed by Tassoni among the best of the author. Muratori does not give it such high praise, although he admits the surpassing beauty of the last tercet, the freshness of the first quatrain, the skill with which Laura is introduced, the nobility of her sentiments, and the high finish of the whole production. With all this commendation, the marvel is that he does not unite with his brother commentator in one general assent of admiration. The last line of the first quatrain may remind the reader of Virgil—

> Ecce supercilio clivosi tramitis undam
> Elicit : illa cadens raucum per levia murmur
> Saxa ciet.

THIRD VARIATION OF THE QUATRAINS.

1 2, 1 2, 2 1, 1 2,
3 4 3, 4 3 4. } Tercets as in Type II.

SONNET CLXXV.—*Non dall' Ispano Ibero all' Indo Idaspe.*

From Spanish Ebro to Hydaspe of Ind,
  Though seeking every bay and shore around,
  From the Red Sea to cliffs which Caspian bind,
  On earth, in heaven is but one Phœnix found.
Shall left hand crow or boding raven sound
  My fate? My life the Sisters how unwind?
  Since ever Pity deaf as asp I find,
  And sorrows, where I hoped for joy, abound.
But not in her alone, in him abide
  Who looks on her, sweet tenderness and love,
  So much she has, there flows from her a tide:
And that my sweetness bitterness may prove
  Cares not, or caring, sympathy would hide
  That Time too soon with grey my hair hath wove.

The commentators are indignant at the irregularity of the quatrains in this sonnet, of which this is a rare example of the author ; and indeed the only specimen of this variation.

As to the interpretation of the sonnet, Tassoni thinks it would puzzle Nævius, the Father of the Augurs, to decide upon it. It has been suggested that Laura may have reminded Petrarch of advancing age by referring to his grey hairs, and that he exclaimed that there was only one Phœnix in the world capable of rising again from its own ashes ; although he, Petrarch, might be regarded as a Phœnix of misery, for his lot was so hard that he found pity deaf in Laura, from whom he hoped to obtain sympathy, since she was so full of sweetness that it overflowed and influenced all who beheld her. But seeing him suffer so that his hair had become prematurely grey, she expressed no sympathy for him. Tassoni, who never shows too much respect for his author, remarks that the poor man was making baths for himself through his grief, *Il povero uomo era andato a' bagni per le doglie.*

Tassoni makes the useless discovery that if the places named in the first quatrain be joined together by lines on a map, they will produce a cross. He also has some learned references on the subject of the augury of birds ; and gravely remarks that the asp is not really deaf, but that it closes its ears against incantations by burying one ear in the ground and stopping the other with its tail. Muratori, referring to this, says that Tassoni does not object to Petrarch's use of the epithet " deaf," " he only makes a physical observation ! "

In conclusion, I may remark that this sonnet is somewhat difficult to translate into English, especially in the same metrical form as the original. This I have attempted. In Bohn's collection an inaccurate translation is given in blank verse. (See page 115 *ante.*)

FIRST VARIATION OF THE TERCETS.

1 2 2 1, 1 2 2 1,
3 4 3, 3 4 3. } Quatrains regular.

SONNET LXXVI.—*Ahi! bella Liberta!*

Alas! fair Liberty, thou'st made it plain,
  In leaving me, what was my state before,
  Ere the first arrow left me stricken sore,
  And gave the wound which may not heal again.
My eyes were so enamoured of that pain,
  That reason's curb availèd me no more;
  They cease to take delight in human lore,
  But as first fascinated, so remain.
For me no pleasure in men's talk is found
  Unless of her, my death. With her loved name
  I fill the air; that name, how sweet the sound!
Love urges not to any path around
  Save that which leads to her; to sing her fame
  Is all my Muse can do—Love sets the bound.

SONNET CIX.—*Amor, che nel pensier mio vive e regna.*

Love, that in all my thoughts both lives and reigns,
  And fills my heart up, as his favourite seat;
  Him armed, and face to face, I sometimes meet;
  Still he dwells there; his ensign there maintains.
She who has taught me love, has taught love's pains;
  And wills that modesty and reverence sweet,
  Should kindled hopes and warm desire defeat,
  Else she my boldness silently disdains.

> Hence Love retreats within my heart for fear,
>   Trembles and weeps, and will attempt no more;
>   And nestling there, refuses to appear.
> What can I do, my guide turned mutineer,
>   Unless to stay with him till life's last hour?
> For he dies well, if love end his career.

Muratori says that it would be difficult to describe in more poetical language the condition of the enamoured poet, accustomed as he was to address Laura modestly and submissively; and if he sometimes ventured to make use of warmer language, the quiet dignity with which she reproved him.

The last line may remind the reader of Propertius, *Laus in amore mori*.

This sonnet formed the subject of a discourse delivered by Michael Angelo before the *Accademia della Crusca*. The discourse is too long (it occupies in my copy fifteen closely-printed quarto pages), and deals too much in minute and verbal criticism, to be of interest to the general reader; but a few extracts may be given with advantage, especially as Michael Angelo was himself a great master of the sonnet. [See Essay, 8, and 12 note.] I must remark, however, that the lecturer's style is so redundant, that I have found condensation to be quite necessary in the translation.

The discourse opens in a strain of pleasant badinage :—" It would be a marvellous and even supernatural thing, most worthy President, and most virtuous Academicians, if any one were to be found so expert in the art of healing as to be able to cure a wound, however slight, in the eye, the heart, or any other more noble part of our body, by the application of a simple argument. So far is such a thing removed from the possible, that, were it accomplished, by so much greater would be the wonder. But in proportion as the object, or rather the subject, is the more estimable, so much the more remarkable would be the artifice referred to; and the greater praise would be due to him who, to the ills of the mind (for such are our vices) were to apply some useful medicine; seeing that the mind is more noble than the body, for this is earthly and corruptible, that celestial and eternal. Hence our Master,

Francesco Petrarca, is worthy of the highest praise and commendation for the charming elegance and good sense that pervade all his poems, calculated as they are to cure the mind of one of its maladies. But I shall endeavour to prove that this especially applies to one of his sonnets, in which, under the discipline of his lady Laura, he persuades with so much gentleness, that any one who, after an attentive study of this short poem, does not become cured, may infallibly despair of his own mental state. Our worthy President, seeing that I languished under such a malady, and had need of a similar cure, and moved by the love that he bears me (for which he has my thanks), thought that he could in some way assist me by requesting me to make a few brief remarks on this sonnet; although in doing so he did not reflect that the attempt would procure but little honour either to him or to me. And you, most courteous Academicians, do not blush for me because I venture to speak on so lofty a theme; nor attribute folly to me, or too much temerity, seeing that I am acting in obedience to him who, by his ample privileges, has full power to command me to embark on this perilous sea; on the waves of uncertain praise, exposed to the winds of ignorance and of censure, which will probably sink me as I go ploughing on with my small bark, handled, as it is, with so little skill. And I trust you will not impute it to me as a fault that there has been so long an interval between the time when I received your commands, and this my attempt to comply with them; since, regarding my small amount of skill, I wished to try to increase it before ascending this rostrum, where I become a sort of town-crier of my own ignorance, and occupy a position which I am so unworthy to fill. Be pleased, therefore, to give me an indulgent hearing for this my brief lecture, and if you should suffer inconvenience in listening to it, you will be pleased to call to mind the inconvenience I have been put to in producing it, contrary to my desire."

He then read the sonnet, and proceeded as follows:—" All things produced by nature are marked by so perfect a foresight and harmony that we are satisfied nothing is made in vain; and that there is no part of any created being that has not its special object. Thus, to note a few examples from terrestrial objects;—fishes and birds have fins and wings, wild beasts limbs, and so on, for every animal ;—while man is endowed with the gift of speech ; so that, unless the fishes, birds, and other animals had been furnished with these members, their several species must have become extinct soon after their creation. So also man without speech, which is his distinctive characteristic, not being able to express his wants, must have remained singularly defective in all his operations. The human mind, which is naturally inclined to imitation, perceiving such exquisite providence in nature, strives to be like her in all the most useful and pleasurable affairs of this life. In this way he generates, as it were, a second nature, which we call *Art*. Now art has divers intentions and ends ; and is varied and divided into different branches, according to the means employed in carrying them out. As the objects of some are more elegant or noble than those of others, so are they esteemed more highly. Others, again, imitate nature under varied conditions, and require that the objects represented should, as it were, appear before the eye just as they do in life, as in sculpture and painting, whence these arts obtain for the most part their highest result, which is the refinement of the affections by the imitation in colour of the actions of men, and of men themselves ; and not only the imitation of nature and of the arts, or other objects which strike the eye, but also those which appeal to the sentiments, as we are informed Aristides the Theban painter knew well how to do ; for in many of his works the actions of the mind and of the senses are expressed in a marvellous manner ; as, for example, in the case of the mother, struck with a mortal blow, thrusting back her child which sought her breast, lest it should imbibe blood instead of milk. With this art of painting poetry is closely allied ; so much so, that painting has often been termed *mute poetry*, and poetry, *eloquent painting*. Hence arises that close friendship between painters and poets, as in the case of Giotto and Dante, Petrarch and Simon of Sienna, which forms no weak illustration of my argument. Not less so is the fact that many who have cultivated poetry have also fortified themselves with the study of painting, as is related of Cratino, the comic poet ; of Dante himself ; and of others in our own time. And this alliance is not only necessary for the sake of the assistance the one obtains from the other, but it naturally arises from the common object of both, which is imitation. They both imitate nature, and the general result is utility, which is gained either by the representation of forms appealing solely to the eye, as in painting ; or appealing both to the eye and the ear, as in poetry. And as Nature is not fallacious in any of her works, so we may learn to read, through the thin veil of fiction, lessons that may inform us, or warn us, according to our need.

" But putting aside for the moment the painter's art, we may remark that our Petrarca, in this sonnet, poetically depicts a lover who, transported by vehement desire and unfounded hopes, is in danger of being caught in the whirlpool of vice and so overwhelmed ; but who, by the penetration and admonitions of the beloved object, corrects himself, and, for fear of offending her, regains a virtuous course. All this is fully expressed in the language of the sonnet, and from it we may derive a lesson of moderation and self-denial.

"*Love, that in all my thoughts, both lives and reigns.*

" So vast and intricate is the forest of amorous science, that whoever ventures into it without the escort of religion soon gets lost in its intricate mazes. Hence many who have attempted to define love have had but an indistinct idea of its varied moods and tenses, and have failed to explain its real nature. Hence, for the sake of clearness, and for the better understanding of this sonnet (which treats of love), it may be convenient to state some of the more obvious forms, without pretending to any very great knowledge on the subject."

He then distinguishes four principal varieties of love ; the first of which, *divine love*, is that which God has for all His creatures, whereby they are maintained and multiplied. The second is *natural love*, or love as it exists in nature (but proceeding, nevertheless, from the divine will), which gives motion to the celestial bodies, such as the revolutions of the heavens and of the planets ; and which also leads earthly objects to exert sympathy, as when plants move towards the sun or the moon, and the like ; or when bodies have some internal relation between them, as the case of the lodestone and iron, or weight and the centre. The third, or *human love*, is that which resides within ourselves, and which manifests itself in the intellect and in the senses. In the intellect it leads us to the contemplation of God, and from His works we learn to love their Creator. Sensual love, which holds a much lower place, leads us to take an interest in pleasing objects, or such as delight the senses. And this kind of love may be purely mental, as when the objects delight the eye or the ear; or it may be corporal and praiseworthy, as in conjugal relations, or otherwise blameable and worthy of punishment. In the fourth place, there is *animal love*, which does not regard the beauty of the object.

Which kind of love influenced our poet there can be no doubt, because, being a man, he could only love as such.

The lecturer goes into a minute analysis of the sonnet, illustrating his remarks by extracts from other parts of Petrarch's Italian poems, and also from Dante, Boccaccio, etc. All this is too long and too minute for insertion here; but I may give the concluding part of the lecture, which refers to the last line of the sonnet—

Che bel fin fa chi ben amando more.

"And this last verse, by its proverbial terseness, makes up the sum of the whole sonnet. We may remark respecting it, that as death is the final termination of this our very short life, so death is good or bad, according to the conduct of the life to which death puts a limit. And as we generally notice those roads which are the most direct and of the best construction lead to inhabited places, while those that are tortuous and rough lead to forests and wild places, so our life, provided it has been conducted with rectitude, will be smooth and delightful in its end; if otherwise, rough and rugged; or, as our poet sings—[1]

> "To gentle souls Death opes the prison drear
> And sets them free; but he is cause of fear
> To those who grovel in the earth, impure.

And so it comes to pass that whoever is conscious in his dying hour of having striven after a good life, feels an inestimable

---

[1] *Trionfo della Morte*, cap. ii.

contentedness, derived, as it is, from the eternal beatitude; while he who has lived dishonestly and viciously must be tormented with the dread of eternal infelicity. Death is, as our poet says,

>Only the breathing of a gentle sigh;

and is, in itself, probably not painful; although an act which deprives us of this our mortal tenement cannot be pleasurable. Nevertheless, whoever passes an honest, praiseworthy life, as he does who adores truth and strives after perfect love; who contemplates God and celestial things; has a due regard for terrestrial ones, which are subject to us, and restrains his appetites by moderation, will arrive at a most peaceful and happy end, as was the case with our poet. Following his example, and cultivating a high and lofty love, we shall pass through the narrow and uncertain passage of death without fear, and become happy, as we know from the teaching of HIM who always was, and always will be, the most munificent benefactor of all who honestly strive after the better way.

"Such is the small amount of seed that I have been able to contribute to this most fertile field, after ploughing it with the ploughshare of my small knowledge." He then thanked the *benignissimi Accademici* for their kindness in being so attentive to his lecture, and thus ended.

First Variation of the Tercets.

1 2 2 1, 1 2 2 1,
3 4 3, 3 4 3. } Quatrains regular.

SONNET CCXLI.   *Alma felice, che sovente torni.*

O happy spirit! deigning to descend
 With consolation for my nights of woe;
 Gazing with eyes not quenched by death, ah no!
 But with earth's beauty, heavenly beauties blend.
What joy that thou consent'st thy aid to lend
 To make my days again in gladness flow;

So that I seem again thy charms to know,
   As if embodied thou didst earthward wend.
Here, where for years I sang thee constantly,
   Now weep thee; but why tell what meets thine eyes?
Weep thee! said I? No! weep the loss to me.
Midst many troubles nought of peace can be,
   Save that at each return I recognise
   By voice, by face, attire, and walking, THEE.

Muratori's comment on this sonnet is instructive, illustrating, as it does, how sensitive the Italian literati are to defects which in a similar production in English would probably escape notice; so little are our poets alive to the conditions required to make a good sonnet. He points out the great beauty of the first quatrain, especially of the third and fourth lines; and also of the first tercet, in which the poet expresses his grief for Laura, and then corrects himself by turning the grief upon himself. In the second quatrain he does not appear to make progress; but repeats less happily the idea of the first. A similar objection applies to the second tercet, which is but a repetition of what has been already said in the second quatrain. Tassoni compares this tercet to an orange which does not yield sweet juice to our pressure; since the consolation that the poet refers to was not simply on account of his recognition of Laura's dress, walk, etc.; but because she appeared to him in her own proper form, as he had already remarked.

Some further observations on this sonnet will be found in the Essay (§ 39, p. 119).

FIRST VARIATION OF THE TERCETS.

1 2 1 2, 1 2 1 2, } Quatrains as in Variation I.
3 4 3, 3 4 3.

SONNET CCLXX. *Quel rosigniuol, che si soave piagne.*

Yon nightingale that thrills out his lament,
   May be for nestlings lost, or consort dear,

> With sweetness fills the air, the plains, intent
> In piteous, varied notes to express his care:
> And all night long his woes with mine seem blent,
> Reminding me too well of my despair.
> The blame was mine so far my folly went,
> I thought a goddess had not death to fear.
> How soon deceived is he who rests secure!
> Who would have thought eyes brighter than the sun
> Could moulder to a little earth obscure!
> And now my cruel loss has made this sure,
> Living and weeping I have had to learn
> That what delights on earth cannot endure.

A tender sweetness pervades the first six lines of this sonnet, which may remind the classical reader of Virgil in the Georgics:—

> *Qualis populea mœrens Philomela sub umbra, etc.*

The author then quits the nightingale, and indulges in a strain of poetical exaggeration. But, as Muratori remarks, an idolater has many privileges. Nevertheless, the melancholy strain of the bird naturally suggests melancholy thoughts to a mind prepared to secrete them.

In the last line of the second quartet I should have preferred to write:—

> To think Death's dart an angel's life would spare!

only the poet has "goddess" (*Dee*).

The second and third lines of the first tercet run thus:—

> *Que' duo bei lumi, assai più che 'l Sol chiari,*
> *Chi pensò mai veder far terra oscura?*

Muratori objects to *far terra oscura* (*fare* being here used in the sense of *divenire* "to become") and would have preferred *far Morte oscuri*; that is, "Who would have believed that Death could have made those bright eyes obscure?"

It is curious to compare the real meaning of the above two lines with the three translations given in Bohn. The first, by Wrangham, is nonsense:—

> "Who would have deemed the darkness, which appears
> From orbs more brilliant than the sun should rise?"

The translator evidently took *terra oscura* for "a darkened world," but how this should arise from brilliant eyes does not appear.

The second (*Anon.* Ox. 1795) is nearer to the original:—

> "Who could have thought that to dull earth would turn
> Those eyes that as the sun shone bright and pure?"

The third is by Charlemont:—

> "The radiance of those eyes who could have thought
> Should e'er become a senseless clod of clay?"

How can "radiance" become a "clod of clay"?

Second Variation of the Tercets.

$$\left.\begin{array}{l}1\ 2\ 2\ 1, 1\ 2\ 2\ 1,\\ 3\ 4\ 5, 5\ 4\ 3.\end{array}\right\}\text{Quatrains regular.}$$

Sonnet LXXII.—*Più volte Amor m'avea già detto: Scrivi.*

> "Write!" is the order Love oft gave to me:
>   "What thou hast seen, in golden letters write:—
>   I make my subjects pale before my sight,
>   And in a moment dead or alive to be.
> Time was, a subject true, I found in thee,
>   And thy example could to lovers cite;
>   And though some higher toil madest thee take flight,
>   Me on the road, to ensnare thee, thou did'st see!
> If the bright eyes I used as my loved throne,
>   From which thou first didst feel my influence high,
>   Making thy heart so hardened, hard no more.
> To me my bow, all conquering, restore,
>   Thou mayst not always boast a tearless eye,
>   For I am fed on tears, as thou must own."

The commentators regard the poetry of this sonnet as being better than its logic. The invention is good, the personification well sustained, and Love speaks with a force and fulness worthy of himself, while the idea that Laura's bright eyes will restore to him his bow is charming. But it is said that the poet is required to write in letters of gold certain of the effects of Love's power ; but why, or wherefore, or whether he obey, we are not told, since Love continues to speak all through the poem. To get over the difficulty, this sonnet is supposed to be meant only as an introduction to the next, Sonnet LXXIII. [See next page.]

Quando giugne per gli occhi al cor profondo.
When mine eyes have thine image inward led.

But it seems to me that the large amount of objection that has been written on this sonnet becomes rather superfluous when we consider the circumstances under which it was written. The poet was about to set out for Rome on public business—and he welcomed such employment, as enabling him the more readily to forget, if not overcome, his passion. Love bids him write about his own power, since, having experienced it, he was the better able to describe it ; and goes on to say that our poet made so good a lover that he was a pattern to other lovers ; but warns him that although he fancies he has shaken off his passion, he will meet him on the road, as he had done aforetime ; or, in other words, the poet will think of Laura's bright eyes, and so Love will recover his bow, that is, re-assume his power ; for the poet knows that although he could forget his passion by keeping his mind employed on other things, yet this was only a temporary resource. All this displays skill and originality, and seems to be sufficiently complete without the prosaic requirements of the commentators above referred to.

Third Variation of the Tercets.

$$\left.\begin{array}{l}1\ 2\ 2\ 1,\ 1\ 2\ 2\ 1,\\ 3\ 4\ 4,\ 4\ 3\ 3.\end{array}\right\}\text{Quatrains regular.}$$

Sonnet LXXIII.

Quando giugne per gli occhi al cor profondo.

When mine eyes have thine image inward led
  To the soul's depths, all others leave the heart;
  The strength that mind to body can impart
Fades, and the limbs seem powerless and dead.
From this first miracle anon is bred
  A second—that which must so depart
  Flies from its home to seize on thee in part,
Gaining revenge, in its own exile glad.
Two faces now assume death's pallid white
  Because the strength which gave to each life's glow
  Nor one nor other has the power to show:
Remembering well what to that day I owe,
  When two so transformed lovers met my sight,
  My own face shows me in the self-same plight.

This is one of Petrarch's obscure sonnets, and as it generally happens, when the tercets are irregularly constructed, by no means one of his best. Nevertheless Tassoni devotes to it several pages of learned comment, with references to Aristotle, Lucretius, and the poetic vision of Plato. The poet seems to imply that in the case of two deeply-smitten lovers there is a sort of mutual transmigration of souls. When the beloved object enters by the eyes into the depths of the heart, it expels all other thoughts and imaginations, and the vital power of the body seems to fade away. This first strange effect, by a kind of reflex action, leads to similar results on the other side, for the mind driven from its own seat partly takes possession of the adored object, and thus, rejoicing in its own exile, takes revenge for being expelled; that is, it produces in the other the same effect that it had itself experienced. Hence both the lovers become pale, etc.

The translation of this sonnet in Bohn is in rhymed couplets. The translator does not seem to have taken sufficient trouble to arrive at the meaning of the sonnet, and hence his result must, I think, be unintelligible to the general reader.

FOURTH VARIATION OF THE TERCETS.

$\left.\begin{array}{l}1\ 2\ 2\ 1, 1\ 2\ 2\ 1, \\ 3\ 4\ 5, 4\ 5\ 3.\end{array}\right\}$ Quatrains regular.

SONNET LXXIV.—*Cosi potess' io ben chiuder in versi.*

Could I embalm, in verse, my thoughts as well
    As in my heart they all embalmèd lie,
    No mortal trained to deeds of cruelty,
But I would make to pity's side rebel.
But ye, bright eyes! whose arrows so assail,
    That shield and buckler every aid deny;
    Without, within, helpless, ye see, am I,
Though I, in open plaints, my griefs ne'er tell.
Since thy keen sight pierces me through and through,
    As the sun's rays light up transparent glass,
    No need that I in words express desire:
Mary and Peter had true faith; alas!
    That my true faith alone should kindle ire,
    And no one understand my case, but thou.

The commentators place this sonnet among the best of the author; although some of them object to the introduction of Mary and Peter—*miscere sacra profanis*; while one commentator, remarking justly the profound reverence uniformly bestowed by our poet on sacred things, bursts out into the following exclamation—"Oh! if Petrarca and Laura were able to return here, and read the doubly distilled nonsense that has been written on his poetry, how they would laugh!"

APPENDIX.

I.—Sestina from Petrarch.

Chi è fermato di menar sua vita.

Who of deliberate choice will spend his life
  Upon the treacherous wave, among the rocks,
Severed from death but by one little ship,
Must count on being always near his end:
Hence, prudent he, who would return to port
While yet the helm has influence o'er the sail. [1]

The gentle gale,[2] to which both helm and sail
  I trusted, entering on my amorous life,
With the full hope to make some better port,
Has led me since among a thousand rocks:
The reasons of my so unhappy end,
As much within were as without my ship.

Shut up for many a day in this blind ship[3]
  I wandered, not once looking to the sail;
And so, before my time, I reached the end:

  The poet, referring to his own life, adopts the metaphor of a ship.

[1] That is, while reason is able to govern passion.
[2] Laura, to whom, on embarking on the sea of love, he submitted both reason and will: hence the danger of being cast upon the rocks —lost in an improper love.
[3] The blind ship, his own body: deceived by his passion and trusting the helm to Love, he is in dread of being wrecked, but it pleased Heaven, etc.

But it pleased Him, to whom I owe my life,
At least so far to free me from the rocks
That in the distant view appeared the port.

As lights by night, bright shining from some port,
   Are sometimes seen at sea by passing ship,
   Unless concealed by tempest or the rocks;
   So I, above my well-inflated sail,
   Saw indications of that other life,[1]
   And then I sighed that I might reach mine end.

Not that I were secure, though at the end,[2]
   But striving while 'tis day to be in port
   Is a long voyage for so short a life.
   And then I fear that in such fragile ship,
   The wind, beyond control,[3] may fill my sail,
   And hurl me forward helpless on these rocks.[4]

Escape I living from these dubious rocks,
   And if my exile[5] have a prosperous end,
   How happy shall I be to furl my sail,
   And cast my anchor in some friendly port;
   Unless I burn, like some ignited ship,
   So hard for me to quit my accustomed life.

Lord of my end, and Lord too of my life,
   Before my ship is wrecked among the rocks,
   Oh, guide to some sure port the much vexed sail![6]

---

[1] He obtains glimpses of the celestial life.

[2] He is not out of danger, seeing that with his frail ship (his weak body) he has yet to make the voyage of life; and, in consequence of his feebleness of purpose, he may be dashed upon the rocks of an irrational life.

[3] The wind—his love for Laura or for the things of this world.

[4] Desirous of celestial good, he fears, nevertheless, that it will be impossible for him to conquer old habits.

[5] He regards life as a state of exile.

[6] The terminal words used in the six preceding stanzas are all brought into the *commiato* according to the law of the sestina. [See Essay, p. 14.]

II.—From Petrarch.

MADRIGAL. } *Perch' al viso d' Amor portava*
1 2 1, 3 2 3, 4 5 4 5. } *insegna.*

Since, in yon pilgrim's face, Love's ensign true
  I see, this foolish heart suggests that I
  No more to other's charms pay reverence due :
And following her upon the verdant grass,
  I heard a loud voice in the distance cry,
  "How many steps in the wood are lost, alas!"
All thoughtful then I sought the shady screen
  Of a tall beech, and gazing all around,
  Marked well how perilous my way had been,
And back, ere half the day had passed, returned.

The poet, fancying he saw in Laura's face some indications of love (Love's ensign true), followed her on the green verdure (that is, where hope seemed to be budding), when he heard a loud voice in the distance (the heaven-born voice of conscience) crying out how men waste their time in this life (the gloomy wood of Dante). Thus admonished, he sought the cool retreat of reason, from which he contemplated his danger, and resolved while yet in middle life to flee from it. This is one of the many indications of Petrarch's resolution to renounce his love for Laura.

III.—From Petrarch.

BALLATA.   }
  1 2 2,   } *Perchè quel, che mi trasse ad amar*
3 4 3 4 4 2 2,   }   *prima.*
5 6 5 6 6 2 2.   }

Though by another's fault, my own first love
  Is ta'en away from me ;
  Yet still I vow to her my fealty.
Amid her golden hair was hid the snare,
  . Which Love about me wound ;

Of those bright eyes, so chill the glances were,
That I, my heart ice-bound,
By virtue of their sudden splendour found;[1]
Hence the mere memory
Causes all other loves save hers to flee!
Now that the auburn tresses I so prize,
I see, alas! no more;
And the sweet glances of those honest eyes,
Departed I deplore;
And since well-dying honour will ensure,
Let Love ne'er set me free
From such a tie, by death or misery.[2]

[1] The three lines terminating here have been misinterpreted by several translators.

E da' begli occhi mosse il freddo ghiaccio,
Che mi passò nel core
Con la virtù d'un subito splendore.

Thus, to give only one example, Dr. Nott has—

"And from those eyes he caught the ray
Which thawed the ice that fenced my breast."

This is quite contrary to the meaning of the original. Ariosto in his 22d sonnet follows Petrarch:—

At the first lightning flashes of thine eyes,
I feel within, without, a freezing cold.

[2] The last three lines are somewhat obscure; but the poet seems to mean that as the loving of a worthy object refines and purifies the soul, he prays Love that he may not be severed from such an object, either by death or suffering.

IV.—FROM PETRARCH.

MADRIGAL. } *Or vedi, Amor, che giovenetta*
1 2 2 1 3 3, 3 4 4. } *Donna.*

Now Love! behold that lady young and fair,
Who scorns thy rule, nor heeds what I endure,
Resting 'twixt two such enemies secure;

Thou armed—she in her robe and flowing hair,
Seated where grass and flowers her bare feet hide;
By her I am unpitied, thou defied.
Her prisoner I; if pity only guide
Thy well-strung bow, and but one arrow thine,
O take revenge for thy sake and for mine.

V.—From Petrarch.

MADRIGAL.
1 2 3, 1 2 3, 4 4. } *Nova angeletta sovra l'ale accorta.*

A beauteous angel, circumspect of wing,
From heaven descended to this verdant shore,
As I passed heedless to my fate unseen.
And seeing me guideless, friendless, wandering,
She stretched a silken snare my way before,
Where the fresh grass had made the pathway green.[1]
Nor did it vex me to be made her prize,
So sweet the light that issued from her eyes.

[1] This is another indication that Petrarch fell in love with Laura not in Avignon, but in the country.—See No. VII.

VI.—On the Literary Habits of Petrarch's Time.

Many passages in Petrarch's letters illustrate the literary habits of his time, and the difficulties of multiplying books before the invention of printing. Petrarch usually kept five or six copyists at work, but, as he remarks in one of his later letters, "now only three, on account of the difficulty of getting good ones. Illuminators are less rare." He frequently complains of the professional scribes—"They promise much, perform little, finish nothing, and spoil all." "If you have not received my verses, it is not on account of my negligence, but of that of the copyists, who constantly disappoint me, so that my studies suffer greatly on their account. They not only break their promises, but keep the trifles entrusted to them, pretending they are lost; so that I must either become their slave or cease to employ them." In apologising to a friend for having kept his Cicero upwards of four years, in order that he might copy it with his own hand, he laments the dearth of copyists capable of understanding such a work. "This occasions great loss to literature, since works already obscure are rendered unintelligible by them. In this way many treasures are lost." In reply to an application for a copy of his treatise *De Vita solitaria* he writes :—" God is my witness, that ten times and upwards I have endeavoured, if the style were not such as to give pleasure to the mind and the ear, that at least the written characters should please the eye ; but all my attempts to overcome the well-known evasions of that part of the literary world known as the copyists, have been vain. It may appear incredible that a work that required only a few months for its composition, cannot be copied in as many years. . . . After many delays, I left it as good as copied in the hands of a priest. I know not whether his promise will be held sacred, as befits his sacred character, or be as fallacious as that of a copyist." In sending his poems to his friend Pandolfo Malatesta, he apologises for the bad writing on account of the difficulty of finding a copyist ; and he remarks on " the scarcity of those who devote themselves to this occupation and their idleness." He also apologises for the binding ; had he not been so far away, the two volumes would have been bound in silver. He adds—" There still remain many other things of mine in the vulgar tongue, but they are so torn that it is difficult to read them. When I happen to have a spare day, I amuse myself in bringing them together ; but this rarely happens. I have ordered some blank leaves to be put at the end of each of the two volumes, and if I succeed in putting together something else, I will send it in separate pages."

Books were so necessary to Petrarch's happiness, that in his frequent travels he gave as a reason for requiring so many horses, that he had to take with him his books. It is to be deplored that the magnificent library presented by him to Venice should have been so little esteemed that in a few years it perished from being kept in a damp room.

It is remarkable how large a portion of their time Petrarch and other literary men devoted to the copying of works of importance. Thus Boccaccio (who was in the habit of lecturing in public on the *Divina Commedia*) sent to Petrarch a copy of Dante's great poem, written entirely in his own hand. Petrarch endeavours to console himself for the labour of copying, by the necessity it imposes for slow and thoughtful reading, " so that in the act of writing many thoughts are suggested that would have been lost by a more rapid method." If the labour became at any time irksome, he called to mind that Cicero copied books with his own hands, in order, as he says, not to be idle on holidays, or days devoted to spectacles.

Letter-writing was also a feature of the age, and took the place of our literary papers and reviews. So eager were people for news, that Petrarch complains of men in Cisalpine Gaul who stopped the couriers, opened the packets, read the letters, and copied whatever took their fancy; and, to save themselves the trouble of copying, they sometimes even kept the packets.

It was also a common practice to commit interesting passages to memory, so that they could be readily reproduced when friends met together. Instead of sending to the library for a volume, as we are accustomed to do, some one was invited to draw upon the treasures of his memory for the entertainment of the company, or for the support of an argument. Thus the history at the end of Boccaccio's *Decameron* " made so lively an impression on me," writes Petrarch, " that I have committed it to memory, in order to retail it sometimes in chatting with my friends."

We get some idea of the mode in which a book was published in the proposal of Coluccio, after Petrarch's death, to revise his Latin poem *Africa*, put a summary at the head of each book, as Ovid had done for the Æneid, and then to get a number of copies made, and send one to Bologna, one to Paris, one to England, and one to Florence, to be deposited in a house to which the public had access.

There seems to be some ground for the idea that Petrarch undervalued Dante's great poem, because it was not written in Latin. He did not even possess a copy until late in life when he received the one from Boccaccio, who in the letter which accompanied it, thought it necessary to explain away some Latin verses in praise of Dante, which he had prefixed to his copy, in order not to wound the susceptibilities of his friend. Petrarch complains of people murdering his Italian verses, and adds—" That is one reason why I renounced the vulgar tongue in which I composed in my youth. I dreaded that which I have seen happen to others, and, above all, to Dante, whose verses I have heard mangled in the public highways and in the theatres; not daring to flatter myself that I could make men's tongues more flexible, and the pronunciation of my verses more sweet. The event proved that I was not wrong. The verses that escaped from me in my youth are in the mouths of the people, who maim them so, that that which I formerly loved now displeases me." . . . " How could I envy Dante, I who do not even envy Virgil? But what do I envy? the hoarse applause of fullers, taverners, butchers, and other people of the like kind, whose praises are an injury rather than an honour? I rejoice in being deprived of such honour, in common with Virgil and Homer." The fact is, that in the long and interesting letter to Boccaccio, from which these extracts are taken, Petrarch seems to place himself above Dante, because he, Dante, seriously devoted his life to writing in the vulgar tongue, which was only the amusement of Petrarch's youth. [See page 161, *ante*.]

Literature received no encouragement from the Church. So ignorant were the higher clergy, that the cardinal, who afterwards became Pope Innocent VI., imagined that Petrarch must be a sorcerer because he read Virgil. A Chartreux monk waited on Boccaccio, and warned him that it had been revealed to one Father Petroni, that unless he, Petrarch, and some others, ceased to write poetry, etc., they would be lost. Boccaccio, in a letter to Petrarch, relates the details of this visit, and asks for advice. Petrarch replies that such things are often done to conceal imposture. " Had the monk paid me a visit, I should have tested his communication by his age, his eyes, his manners, his dress, his general appearance, his mode of sitting down, his voice, his address—all these things would have enlightened me. . . . Literature is not an obstacle to holiness. There are many roads to heaven, long and short, bright and obscure, high and low. Ignorance is the route taken by the idle; nevertheless, the sciences can produce as many saints as ignorance; and we must beware how we compare an ignorant devotion with an enlightened piety."

VII.—On the Identification of Laura.

It still remains a literary problem of high interest, as it respects the character of a great and good man and a pure writer, whether the Laura of Petrarch and the Laura of the Abbé de Sade are identical. During upwards of four centuries the common belief was that Laura was never married, but in 1764 the Abbé published, at Amsterdam, in two large 4to volumes, and in 1767 a third volume, his skilful and amusing *Mémoires pour la vie de F. Petrarque*. In this extensive work, in which the archives of the De Sade family appear to have been thrown open for the first time, the Abbé endeavours to prove that Laura de Noves was the daughter of Audibert de Noves, a gentleman of Provence, that she was born at Avignon in 1307 or 1308, was married in January 1325 to Ugo de Sade, a noble citizen of that place, was first seen by Petrarch in 1327, two years after her marriage, in the Church of Santa Clara in the same city, where she died of the plague on the 6th April 1348, having been the mother of seven sons and four daughters.

This theory, supported as it is by a large number of family and other documents, and by much acute reasoning, made a profound impression at the time, and has been, with some exceptions, generally accepted ever since. Gibbon gave it his powerful support in a note appended to the last chapter but one of the Decline and Fall, and one of the latest writers of authority, Ugo Foscolo (1823), also adopted it; since which the biographical notices of the poet that have appeared in our cyclopædias, etc., and separately, such as that by Thomas Campbell, have adopted De Sade's theory.

And yet it is surprising that little or no notice should have been taken of a work by one of Campbell's countrymen, namely, Alexander Fraser Tytler, afterwards Lord Woodhouselee, who, in 1784, published a pamphlet in refutation of De Sade's theory, and also, in the fourth volume of the "Transactions of the Royal Society of Edinburgh," "A Dissertation on an Historical Hypothesis of the Abbé de Sade." A fuller statement appeared in 1812, entitled "An Historical and Critical Essay on the Life and Character of

Petrarch." Some Italian writers also took up the subject, among whom may be mentioned Professor Marsand, who had the honour of restoring to its integrity the text of Petrarch's poems, and who states at the end of his *Biblioteca Petrarchesca* (p. 231) that he had prepared a refutation of De Sade's theory, but threw it aside on reading the masterly essay of Lord Woodhouselee.

I may also refer to the historical notes appended to the fourth canto of Lord Byron's "Childe Harold," by Mr. Hobhouse. In his annotation on the 25th stanza, which ends with the couplet,

"Watering the tree which bears his lady's name
With his melodious tears, he gave himself to fame,"

he says:—"Thanks to the critical acumen of a Scotchman, we now know as little of Laura as ever. The discoveries of the Abbé de Sade, his triumphs, his sneers, can no longer instruct or amuse."

It must not, however, be supposed that no researches had been made as to who Petrarch's Laura really was until the Abbé's theory was promulgated. As early as 1520, Velutello, in his notice of the poet prefixed to his annotated edition of the Italian poetry,[1] made some remarks on the subject. He was informed by a very old man, named Gabriel de Sade, who claimed to be descended from Ugo, brother of John de Sade, father of Laura, of Gravesons, a property of the family, where she was born, that she was living between 1360 and 1370; but this date not coinciding with the Laura of Petrarch, he searched the parish registers in the neighbourhood of Vaucluse, and found an entry of Laura, daughter of Arrigo di Chiabau, signor of Cabrières, baptized 4th June 1314, and that she died there, and was buried at the Franciscan Church of Lisle, close to Cabrières and Vaucluse, to which the people of those places were accustomed to go to mass.

Now it is contended that Laura di Chiabau, who was

---

[1] Velutello is one of the most judicious of Petrarch's commentators, and has furnished later writers with a good deal of material. I have a copy of his book, a new and enlarged edition, Venice, 1552, containing about 330 leaves.

born, and lived and died, at Cabrières, and was never married, is the Laura of Petrarch.

This theory has been adopted by many writers, and has also been opposed; the chief points of opposition being the doubt as to whether there were any baptismal registers in the fourteenth century; and also whether at that time Cabrières was anything more than a waste, uninhabited place. Moreover, if Laura was born in 1314, and Petrarch first met with her in 1327, as we know from his 176th Sonnet, Laura could have been only between twelve and thirteen years of age; whereas, in the imaginary dialogue with St. Augustin, the saint says that Petrarch is only a few years older than Laura—" si vero paucorum numerus annorum quo illam præcedis," and it is contended that ten years in the course of a human life would not be called a few years older. But, in answer to this, the sestina *Anzi tre dì*, etc., according to the judgment of the best commentators, makes Laura, when Petrarch first saw her, to be only twelve or thirteen years of age; and in this poem she is referred to as a " tender flower," *tenero fiore*, which is more applicable to a young girl than to a woman of nineteen or twenty, and who, according to De Sade's theory, was married and already a mother.

So much as to Laura's age; next as to the place of her birth. In the 264th Sonnet the poet invokes the beatified spirit of Laura to look upon him in compassion while he is wandering sorrowfully on the banks of the Sorga; but not to look upon her birthplace (Cabrières) near the source of the river, nor upon the adjoining meadow where their love commenced, because he would not remind her of that which had been a source of vexation to her, namely, to have been born in so humble a place. So also, in the *Trionfo della Morte*, Laura says—

> Displeased am I, as it respects myself,
> That I was born in so obscure a place.

That is, she imagined that, having become the theme of so much beautiful poetry, she ought to have had a more exalted birthplace, such, in fact, as Avignon would have been.

In the 247th Sonnet, *I' ho pien di sospir*, etc., the poet climbs the hills of Vaucluse to look down upon the lovely plain " where she was born, who held in her hand my heart, both in its time of flowering and of fruiting." The lovely plain here referred to must be Cabrières ; it could not have been Avignon, for that is fifteen miles off, and not visible from Vaucluse ; moreover, it could not be called " a lovely plain."

In the 260th Sonnet, also written at Vaucluse, the poet expressly points to the spot from which " her naked spirit ascended to heaven, leaving its lovely tenement to earth a spoil." That is, she died in her father's house at Cabrières, and not in Avignon.

Between these two events, namely, the birth and the death of Laura, there are numerous passages which associate her life with the objects in and around Vaucluse, forming a body of internal evidence which ought surely to outweigh the external and inferential evidence collected so assiduously by an interested witness, even supposing him to have been honest, who was anxious to connect with his own family name the name of a lady rendered famous by Petrarch's poetry.

Now this poetry is so intensely personal, and the character of the poet so thoroughly honest and straightforward, that any evidence derived from it ought to have great weight. Even where the treatment is allegorical, the poet is still dealing with his own personal history, thoughts, and feelings, and there is no difficulty in tracing them.

Were I to discuss all the points of this controversy, this note would assume the dimensions of a volume. Enough will have been done to vindicate Petrarch's character if it can be proved that his Laura was never married. All that De Sade proves is that there was a married lady of Avignon named Laura, but he does not prove that she was Petrarch's Laura.

I propose to examine briefly what De Sade considers to be the strong points of his theory.

I. In his Latin, as in his Italian, writings, Petrarch refers to Laura as *mulier, fœmina, donna, madonna*, terms applicable to a married woman ; and not as *virgo, puella, vergine, donzella*, etc., which he would have done had Laura been unmarried.

The Abbé here overshoots the mark, and proves too much, seeing that Dante, Cino, and all the poets of that time, as well as the poets of a later period, Tasso, Ariosto, etc., address their ladies as *Donna* and *Madonna*, in cases where they are known to refer to unmarried women ; and Zotti, in his edition of Petrarch (iii. 242), gives a number of cases, and, among others, from the Roman law, to prove that *mulier* and *fœmina* are equally applicable to unmarried and married women. But in one of his Eclogues (the eighth) Petrarch does refer to Laura under the term *puella* (which, however, proves nothing, seeing that the term also applies to young married women); but in the third Eclogue, in relating the story of his love to Daphne (the Laurel), he says he has wooed her during fifteen years, and that she is still free—

Tu cui libertas salva est tibi consule Daphne.

See also the 157th Sonnet, *Una candida cerva*, etc., APPENDIX, No. VIII., page 223, and note, page 224, *postea*.

II. De Sade says that when Petrarch describes the dress of Laura, it is that of a married woman, to whom rich dresses, tiaras of gold, pearls, etc., were limited; while unmarried women were made to dress much more simply.

Here, again, the Abbé proves too much, for, according to his view, Laura must have been unmarried when Petrarch first met with her, when "her golden hair was streaming in the wind;" but it is not true that rich attire was limited to married women, seeing that during the pontificate of Clement VI. a decree was published prohibiting the use of gold, silver, ermine, and silk, in the dresses of all females, except the relatives of the Pope, the wives and daughters of marshals, barons, etc. Moreover, in the 163d Sonnet, the poet again refers to Laura, who once wore her hair loose but now confines it with pearls and gems, which formed a common difference between a young girl of rank and one some years older; so that here is an additional evidence that Petrarch knew Laura when she was unmarried. Indeed, he refers to her as "the young damsel, who now is a woman,"

La bella giovenetta ch' ora è donna,

as if he would say that he knew her as a girl, when she dressed as became her age; and that, now she is a woman, she dresses according to her age and rank; but the line just quoted does not, as De Sade supposes, refer to her unmarried and married condition. [See Canzone, *In quella parte*, Stanza II.]

III. The Abbé says that had Laura been unmarried, the "Triumph of *Chastity*" would have been the "Triumph of

Virginity" (which does not at all follow), and the poet would have given her virgins as companions, instead of matrons. This is simply a misstatement, since, in the poem in question, Virginia, the nine Muses, and one of the vestal virgins, are introduced; and he says, moreover,

Io non poria le sacre benedette
Virgini ch' ivi fur, chiuder in rime.

(I am not able to include in my rhymes the sacred blessed virgins who were here.)

But if the married or unmarried condition of Laura is to be determined by her companions, it would be easy to give instances in which Laura is surrounded by unmarried women; as in the 11th Eclogue, in which the companions of Laura weep for her under the name of Galatea, and it is said that she is gone to increase the assembly of the virgins (Virgineos addam cœtus).

IV. The Abbé's strongest point is this. In the third imaginary dialogue with St. Augustin, the Saint reasons with the poet on the folly of placing his affections upon an object of which death may deprive him. The poet replies that he hopes he shall not live long enough to see the day of her death; and remarks that, in the course of nature, Laura being younger than he, she ought to survive him. To this St. Augustin replies that, nevertheless, her death is very probable, seeing that her fair body has lost much of its pristine vigour by reason of disease, as well as frequent perturbations. ("Quod corpus illud egregium morbis ac crebris perturbationibus exhaustum, multum pristini vigoris amisit.")

Now, in all the early printed copies of Petrarch's works, the word *perturbationibus* is printed in full, or with only a slight contraction *pturbationibus*, as in the Venice edition of 1501, now before me; or *pturbationib.*, in the Basle editions of 1496 and 1554. And it is perfectly clear that the manuscripts from which these editions were printed must have had the words as above given, for we cannot suppose that it would be left to the discretion of the compositor to make any considerable contraction. But De Sade says that in the Royal Library of Paris were two manuscripts in which the word in question is not *perturbationibus*, but simply a contraction, *ptubs.*, which, according to him, should be read *partubus*, or "child-bearing," so that "her constitution was exhausted by frequent child-bearing." If this really were the meaning, there would no longer be any doubt about Laura's married or unmarried condition; but seeing that not one of the early printed copies supports this view, we must suppose that most of the MSS. were like the early printed copies, and represented the common reading. Even could it be proved that the two MSS. in question were the earliest in existence (one of them Petrarch's original copy, for example), and that the copyists of subsequent manuscripts expanded the contraction *ptubs.* into *perturbationibus*, and that from one of these the dialogue was afterwards set up in type, De Sade would not prove his theory; for it would still be as much unsettled as ever as to what the author really meant by *ptubs.*

The poet's reply to the Saint's remark is omitted by De Sade. It is this—"Et ego quoque et curis gravior et ætate provectior factus sum." "I also am laden more heavily with cares, and am more advanced in years." In this reply *curis* naturally goes with *perturbationibus*, but would be ridiculous with *partubus*.

De Sade does not say that he saw the two manuscripts in the Royal Library, but he quotes a certificate from the librarian Capperonier, who certifies not enough, and yet too much; for he quotes the MSS. as they *ought* to be read "on lit, et qu'on doit lire," "et corpus illud egregium morbis ac crebris partubus exhaustum," etc.; whereas De Sade distinctly says that *partubus* is not to be found in these MSS., but the contraction *ptubs.*, which he interprets into *partubus*.

The writings of Petrarch were held in such high esteem that a very large number of copies were scattered over Europe, most of which were probably of about Petrarch's time; for within sixty-six years of his death printing put an end to copying; and it is not probable that so important a word as the one in question should have been left to the mercy of a doubtful contraction, but rather its meaning, as given in the printed copies, was so well understood that a contemporary of Petrarch would have had no difficulty in reading for *ptubs.* the word as printed. We must also suppose the early printers to have been more skilful in interpreting the abbreviations of MSS. than a man who comes four hundred years later, and gives a meaning which is altogether opposed to the reading of the printed copies.

In answer to the objection that so long a word was not likely to be contracted into *ptubs.*, it may be stated that different MSS. give the contraction differently. In one MS. in the Laurentian library, according to Baldelli, an *i* is introduced, which is not found in *partubus;* and in another an *a*, *patubs.*, which is. But the MSS. of the thirteenth and fourteenth centuries exhibit such frequent mistakes that no argument ought to be based upon the variation of a word made by one of the copyists. They contracted as it suited their pleasure or their interest; they followed no rule, the most expeditious method being the best. That they were a slovenly, dishonest set of men, is evident from Petrarch's frequent complaints respecting them, some of which are quoted in the preceding note, No. VI.

The Abbé has a remark on the word *crebris*, as being applicable to *partubus*, but not to *perturbationibus*, to which *multis* would, he thinks, apply; but it has been shown that the best authorities use *creber* in the sense of *frequens* or *assiduus*, and that it is more correct than *multus*.

V. I come now to one of the most incredible of all the Abbé's statements. It is said that in 1533 (that is, 185 years after Laura's death) a tomb was discovered in the church of the Cordeliers at Avignon, in one of the chapels containing the family vault of the De Sades. On raising the stone, which had no inscription, nothing was at first discovered except earth mingled with bones; but on a closer search, a casket of lead, bound with a wire of brass, was found, containing a piece of vellum folded, and sealed with green wax, and also a bronze medal, on one side of which was the figure of a very little woman, surrounded by four letters M. L. M. I., which were supposed by some to be the initials of the inscription *Madonna Laura morta jace*. The parchment contained writing that was scarcely legible; but, in the clear light of the sun, a sonnet was made out, beginning

Qui riposan quei caste e felici ossa.
Here rest those chaste and happy bones.

These statements depend on the authority of a Florentine,

named Mannelli, who, aided by two others, made the search in question, being guided thereto by the MS. note said to have been written by Petrarch in his copy of Virgil. [See Part I. § 23.] But to say nothing of the extreme improbability of written characters, in a damp tomb, remaining legible after two centuries, Italian critics of repute are agreed that the sonnet in question could not have been written by Petrarch, its style being so different—so very inferior, containing, as it does, senseless rhymes, and even ungrammatical structure. As to the note in the Virgil, so much turns upon its authenticity that I shall return to it presently.

The persons who made these discoveries in the tomb in 1533 did not publish any account of them until 1550, or seventeen years later; and the narration is, to say the least, very improbable. The manuscript note in Virgil, the sonnet, and the medal, bear conflicting testimony. If the note in Virgil be authentic, the sonnet and the medal fall under suspicion; if these be authentic, then the note in Virgil cannot be admitted. According to the note, Laura died in Avignon on the 6th April, and was buried the same day, a necessary precaution in the case of persons dying of the plague. The burial must have been hasty, at a time when all were made anxious by the pestilence, and no one knew who would be the next victim. Was that a time to think of sonnets and medals? or rather, was there time to prepare them in the few hours that intervened between the death and the burial? and it was not probable that the authorities would allow the tomb of a person who had died of the plague to be reopened in order to deposit a leaden casket. According to the note, Petrarch was at Verona when Laura died, and heard the news a week later at Parma. If this, then, be the tomb of Laura, and the sonnet and the medal were found in it, she could not have been buried on the same day that she died, and the account given in the note in Virgil is not true. There are other difficulties. If the letters on the medal really imply *Madonna Laura morta jace*, why put the inscription inside where no one could see it, and not outside, in the usual place. If J can be taken for *jace* (although the Italians do not use *jace* for *giace*) something is wanting to indicate *Qui* "here," if it be an Italian inscription, or *Hic*, if it be a Latin one, in which case the J would represent *jacet*. Tomasini gives a copy of the medal, with the letters M. L. M. L. (not I.) But whatever the letters, they may be interpreted in a number of ways to suit almost any theory.

Next, as to the note in Virgil: Bruce Whyte,[1] who examined it, with the assistance of two experts, states that it is written in a style of extraordinary simplicity, a quality not characteristic of the Latin compositions of Petrarch. Moreover, on comparing the handwriting with specimens of the poet's writings known to be authentic, differences were observed in certain letters, sufficient to throw a certain amount of suspicion on the authenticity of the note. It was also discovered that the first word *Laura* was written with a double *r*, so as to make *Laurra*, a mistake not likely to have been committed by Petrarch; and, further, that a clumsy attempt had been made to convert one of the *r*'s into an *e*, so as to make *Laurea*. Mr. Whyte justly considered this of sufficient importance to request the two librarians who assisted him in the examination to furnish him with a certificate, which he prints, recording the fact.

A *facsimile* of the note is given by Marsand in his splendid edition of the *Rime* (Florence, 1822); but several authorities agree that the handwriting of Petrarch's time embarrasses every one on the question of identity. The book has often changed hands from the time when the Dondi family possessed it, in 1380 or 1390, until it found a safe asylum, first in the Library of Pavia, afterwards in the Ambrosian Library of Milan, where it remained undisturbed, if we except a forced visit to Paris in the time of the first Napoleon. In 1795 the book was pulled to pieces, and other notes by Petrarch were found, recording the deaths of many of his friends, such as that of Paganini in 1348, the year of Laura's death, but not her death. Hence it has been supposed that Petrarch wrote a short note on paper, intending to expand it at some future time, but not having done so, it was recast, with interpolations, by one of the early possessors of the book. Vitalis[2] gives an account as to how mistakes

---

[1] "Histoire des Langues Romanes et de leur Litterature." Paris, 1841. See vol. iii. ch. xxxviii.

[2] See Vitalis, "Les Environs de Vaucluse." 1842.

may thus have arisen without any intention to deceive ; but for this I must refer to his book, fully agreeing with his conclusion that Petrarch's works manifestly contradict the note in Virgil as to the place of first meeting with Laura ; and that there is no doubt about the authenticity of the poems, but great doubt as to the authenticity of the note.

As there are many passages in Petrarch's works which distinctly refer to her birthplace, so there are passages which define her place of burial. In the 11th Eclogue, in which Laura is celebrated under the name of Galatea, three nymphs are introduced, one of whom asks the others to describe where Galatea is buried. The description is sufficiently rural. But without quoting further on this point, it may be stated that numerous passages in the works of Petrarch bear concordant testimony to the points insisted on in this argument. It is not pretended that the evidence is more than inferential; but on the other hand it is not beset with the difficulties that surround the various points of De Sade's theory, when they come to be closely examined.

The extreme improbability of this theory suggests several other considerations. Is it likely that the wife of a nobleman, living in so important a city as Avignon, could have been the object of adoration on the part of so celebrated a man as Petrarch ; that his sonnets in her praise should be poured out by hundreds, and sung in the streets over Italy, if not Europe, and the lady herself be so far unknown that a member of the Colonna family, namely, the Bishop of Lombes, as already noticed (Part I. § 17), not only did not know her, but supposed her to be a creation of the poet's fancy ; while the poet's most intimate friend, Boccaccio, referred to her as an allegory of the laurel crown ? Would it be likely that no contemporary writer should have mentioned her ? Would her husband have permitted all these glowing effusions to be circulated respecting his wife ? Had she been a wife and a mother, would Petrarch never have alluded to the fact ? He describes the most minute particulars respecting her, such as her gown, her glove, her veil, her jewels, her mirror, her window, her walking, sitting, musing, singing, talking ; he describes her alone and in company ; in smiles, in tears, in sickness, and in health ; but he never once refers to her husband and children. He rewards the artist who painted Laura's portrait with a couple of sonnets, but there are no birth or birthday sonnets in honour of Laura's children. After her death, the poet is in frequent communication with her spirit, and still there is no reference to her children; but the style of conversation is just such as might be expected between two lovers who could not be united on earth, but hoped for union in heaven.

There is a want of agreement in the portraits of Laura, three of which are distinguished among a crowd of others, and these three do not resemble each other. It is not likely that Simon could have taken Laura's portrait for Petrarch under the eye of a jealous husband, or without his knowledge, seeing that the two sonnets above referred to would have divulged the secret. It is probable that at the time Simon was employed, Petrarch was at Vaucluse, and Laura at Cabrières. This portrait was painted in 1338-9.

Then there is the extreme improbability of a man of such strong religious convictions as Petrarch paying court to a married woman. In the 288th Sonnet he speaks in terms that are quite irreconcilable with the theory that he did so :—

> *S' onesto amor può meritar mercede.*
> If honest love may merit a reward.

Love for a married woman would not be honest; nor could he say that "his faith to her, like the bright sun, was known to all the world;" nor call on Heaven to bear witness to its purity, Laura now in heaven knowing that it was pure. Had this been a guilty love, he could not have concluded this sonnet with the following tercets :—

> May she, at length, from Heaven compassionate
> Give ear to all my sighs, soothe me to rest
> With visions of herself in sympathy :
> And when, at last, I quit this mortal state,
> May she conduct me to the spirits blest,
> True friends of Christ, true friends of honesty.

I may also refer to the 305th Sonnet, commencing thus :—

> Methinks the messenger each hour I hear,
> That Laura sends to call me to her side.

And concluding thus—

> Happy the day of my escape, when I
> From this poor mortal prison-house get free,
> And its frail scattered ruins leave behind;
> Cleaving the darkness that oppresses me,
> Into the bright serene I upwards fly,
> And there my Saviour and my Lady find.

But supposing the main points of De Sade's theory to have been disposed of, and it is admitted that Laura was never married, it is difficult to understand the hopeless passion of Petrarch. If the poet knew that she could frown, he has frequently told us of her smile. Why then were they not married? So far as I have been able to form an opinion on the subject, the answer is likely to flow from two sources:—1. The peculiar position of Petrarch with respect to the Church; 2. The peculiar character of Laura. With respect to the first, Petrarch was an ecclesiastic belonging to the secular clergy, wearing the tonsure and the clerical dress, and holding several benefices that did not involve the cure of souls. He held a canonry in Cavaglione; he was archdeacon of the Cathedral of Parma; canon in the Cathedral of Padua; domestic chaplain to Robert, King of Naples; and was even offered a bishopric. He was a favourite with several of the Popes, who were desirous to engage his services in the pontifical secretaryship. Squerciafico and other early biographers state that one of the Popes (Castrucci says it was John XXII., who was elected 1316, and died 1334) wished Petrarch to marry Laura, and offered him his apostolical dispensation, together with certain rich benefices; but that our poet refused, with the remark, *Non volo divenir marito per non lasciare d'essere amante*,—" I wish not to become a husband, in order that I may not cease to be a lover." But when Petrarch first met Laura he was an exile, without fortune, and could not aspire to the hand of the daughter of a nobleman, or rather her family would have opposed such a mesalliance. Secondly, Laura's character, as we are repeatedly assured by the poet, had in it something that belonged rather to heaven than to earth; and in the dialogue with St. Augustin already referred to, she is described as having her mind disengaged from the cares of this world, burning as she is with heavenly desires,—" Cujus mens, terrenarum nescia curarum, cœlestibus desideriis ardet." These few words seem to explain as religious excitements the *perturbationibus* already referred to, and would also incline Laura to regard her tonsured admirer as a priest with whom marriage would be sacrilege. This would explain the cold looks and high disdain by which she kept him at a distance when his advances were too eager ; and it would not oppose an occasional smile by way of retaining-fee for him who sang her charms in such beautiful verses. The priest on one side, and the nobleman's daughter on the other, might occasionally meet on the tacit understanding that they were lovers, although their respective social positions prevented a closer relationship. That they thus met is evident from the *Rime*, which also bear witness to their jealousies, and estrangements, and reconciliations, their meetings at indoor parties, water parties, and garden parties ; and at one of these last, the owner gathered two roses, and presenting one to each, remarked, "The sun never shone upon such a pair of lovers" (Sonnet CCVII., *Due rose*). That Laura was under parental authority is evident from Sonnet CLXIII., *L' aura serena*, in which the poet complains that she is kept from him by disdain (*sdegno*) ; and again, in Sonnet CLXXXVI., *Liete e pensose*, when some ladies inform him that Laura is not allowed to join their party, as usual, lest she should meet her lover, he exclaims indignantly, "Who shall restrain lovers, or impose laws on them !" The ladies reply, that although her body may be held captive her mind is free. When Charles of Luxemburg saluted Laura in public [ESSAY, § 24], the poet is filled with envy at the act, "so sweet and strange," (Sonnet CCI., *Real natura*). And, lastly, in Sonnet CCLXXIV., *Tutta la mia fiorita etade*, when the poet, now high in rank and importance, seems to have overcome Laura's scruples, or those of her friends, and marriage seemed possible, envious death took her away. All this is consistent with the theory that Laura was not married, but it is inconsistent with De Sade's theory.

VIII.—Allegory on Laura.

Sonnet CLVII. }   *Una candida cerva sopra l' erba.*
Type I.

At sunrise, while the season yet was cold,
  Between two rivers, 'neath a laurel shade,
  Appeared to me upon the verdant glade,
  A fair white hind; her horns were both of gold:
So sweetly proud she seemed, as ne'er was told,
  That I, to follow her, all work delayed;
  As when the miser some new gain has made,
  For joy forgets his labours manifold.
This motto round her collar, sparkling bright,
  In diamond and topaz, I espied:
  LET NO ONE TOUCH ME—CÆSAR HAS MADE ME FREE.
And now the sun had reached his noontide height:
  Weary with gazing, but not satisfied,
  I saw no more, the abyss received me.

In this allegory the poet refers to his first meeting with Laura in early spring, at sunrise, on the 6th April 1327. The snow-white hind refers to her fair person and pure mind, and the horns of gold indicate her hair. The place of meeting was between the two rivers, Rodono (the Rhone) and Druenza, that is between Vaucluse and Lilla (L'Isle); and the laurel shade signifies that the body of Laura overshadowed or veiled her mind. In the second quatrain, the figure of the miser is not well sustained. The poet relates that the vision had such an effect upon him that he gave up all other work in order to follow it; but he says that the miser forgets the toil in the pursuit of gain. With respect to the collar, the ancients, and after them the alchemists, attached many virtues to precious stones, the diamond protecting the wearer from the allurements of love, and the topaz conferring coldness.[1] The motto signifies that it had pleased God to make the wearer free from all carnal desires and imperfections. The sun had now attained his meridian; that is, a life of seventy years is represented by a day, and Laura died before she had completed half her day, or middle life;[2] or, as she says elsewhere (Sonnet CCLXI., Part II., p. 156, *ante*),

And closed my day, before the eve was near.

The poet gazed in rapture so long as the beautiful vision remained in sight, but when it disappeared, he fell into the abyss of grief. It is impossible to apply all this to a married woman.

Although this Sonnet is included in the *Vita*, and may have been written while Laura was sick and in apprehension of her death (see Sonnet CCXI., Part I., page 132), it may also have been written after her death, seeing that her age at the time of that event is so nearly indicated.

The Sonnet seems to have been based upon a story related of Cæsar, who set at liberty some deer, with a circlet of gold round the neck of each, containing the motto—*Noli me tangere, quia Cæsaris sum*—" Let no one touch me, because I belong to Cæsar."

---

[1] In the "Triumph of Chastity" Laura is described as being dressed in white, to denote her purity, with a chain of diamonds and topazes round her neck, with which love was effectually bound; and it is stated that ladies now have no such strong chains wherewith to bind love. In the "Triumph of Death"

La bella Donna e la compagne elette

are described as being dressed in green, the colour of spring, emblematical of youth, and round their neck white ermine, with gold and topazes, emblems of their purity, modesty, and candour.

[2] This agrees much better with Velutello's date (page 210) than with De Sade's (page 209):—

	De Sade.	Velutello.
Laura died	1348	1348
was born	1307	1314
Laura's age	41	34

It is obvious that thirty-four is more appropriate to *mezzo giorno* (middle age) than forty-one.

IX.—German Translations of Petrarch's Sonnets.

Among the German translators of Petrarch's sonnets are Förster (Leipzig, 1851), Krigar (Hannover, 1866), and Hübner (Berlin, 1868). This last, however, is a selection of one hundred and fourteen sonnets, which, according to Geiger (Petrarka, Leipzig, 1874), are so admirably translated, as to throw all previous attempts into the shade. I have read them with great interest, and find their chief merit to consist in their poetical ring (which is so rare a quality in translations). In producing it, M. Hübner has been assisted not only by a good ear but by the judicious admixture of male and female rhymes, which give his language so much advantage over our own.[1] In common with most other translators he takes great liberties with the form, especially in the grouping of the tercets. He generally succeeds in keeping the quatrains regular, although in some cases these are varied in a most objectionable manner; as, for example, in Sonnet 233, *Datemi pace*, 1 2 2 1, 3 2 2 3; in Sonnet 198, *O Cameretta*, 1 2 2 1, 1 3 3 1; and in Sonnet 315, *Spirto felice*, 1 2 2 1, 3 4 4 3. He is still more irregular in the tercets, which, in some cases, assume very objectionable forms, introducing rhymed couplets 3 3 4, 3 3 4, and such eccentric groupings as 3 4 3, 5 4 5, and 4 5 6, 4 6 5. In fact, the author thinks it necessary to apologise for the liberties he has occasionally taken with the form.

But faults of a graver character are to be occasionally met with, such as mistranslations, omissions, and interpolations, and want of perception as to the point of the sonnet. In Sonnet CLVII., *Una candida cerva* [see page 223, *ante*], the translation begins with the last line of the first quatrain—

> *Levando 'l sole alla stagione acerba.*
> At sunrise, in the season immature;

i.e. in early spring; but M. Hübner has got—

> *Es war im Frühling und der Tag war heiss.*
> It was in spring-time, and the day was hot.

---

[1] The *männliche Reim* consists of one rise or one fall, such as *lang, Gang, Gesang*. The *weibliche* is made up of one rise and one fall, such as *gelingen, singen, klingen*.

The translator says nothing about sunrise, and Petrarch does not say that the day was warm. But there is a still graver fault of omission. The translator omits three lines of the second quatrain, including the simile of the miser; transfers the first tercet to the second quatrain; and makes up his two tercets with the assistance of padding. Petrarch occasionally drops, in a quiet way, two or three words, which the careless reader might pass over as expletives, but which really form the key-note of the poem. For example, in Sonnet LXIX., *Erano i capei* [see page 177, *ante*], the poet, many years after his first meeting with Laura, describes her charms as he saw them for the first time, and winds up the sonnet with the beautiful figure of the slackened bow. But in the first quatrain the poet just drops a hint that the lustre of Laura's eyes is now somewhat dimmed, which gives point and force to the closing simile. But M. Hübner omits these pregnant words, and instead of the bright light that once flashed from Laura's eyes, *but now dimmed*, he substitutes the words, *die wie Sterne stehen*, "which stand out like stars." Petrarch, in winding up the sonnet, again drops two or three words—*e se non fosse or tale*—"and if they" [her charms] "are no longer such" [as above described],

The slackening of the bow heals not the wound.

But, by a singular perversity, M. Hübner again omits the few pregnant words which are so necessary to the point of the sonnet. The following is the last tercet in the original, with the German and the English translations:—

Uno spirto celeste, un vivo Sole
Fu quel ch' i' vidi; e se non fosse or tale,
Piaga per allentar d' arco non sana.

Ein Himmelsgeist, lebend 'ger Sonne Regung
War, was ich sah; so bleibt die Liebeswunde
Ob schlaff der Bogen, ohne Linderungen.

A heavenly spirit did I see and hear,
A living sun; and if such charms take wing,
The slackening of the bow heals not the wound.

As a specimen of M. Hübner's best style, I give the following from Sonnet CCLXX., *Quel rosigniuol* [see page 194, *ante*]. It is easy and flowing, and its faults are due to the necessities of rhyme. In the third line, for example, the original says that the nightingale fills with sweetness the sky and the country round; the translator says, "fills the sky night and day;" and in the fifth line he says "night" only; and omits the word that describes the variety of the bird's notes. Such faults as these disfigure more or less all the efforts of this otherwise meritorious translator :—

> Die Nachtigall, die mit so holder Klage
>   Um Kind und Gattin trauert, ihre Lust
>   Erfüllt mit Sang den Himmel Nacht und Tage
>   Im seelenvollsten Ton der kleinen Brust.
> Sie klagt mit mir die Nacht, als ob sie trage
>   Wie ich den schwersten, schmerzlichsten Verlust,
>   Wenn ich mir weinend immer wieder sage:
>   "Dass Engel sterben hab' ich nicht gewusst!"
> Wie irrt' ich schwer, da ich so sicher war,
>   Dass ihre schönen Augen, hell wie Sterne,
>   Nie könnten dunkel, Staub und Asche werden!
> Jetzt erst erkenn' ich, ach und seh' es klar,
>   Mein Schicksal will, dass ich in Thränen lerne,
>   Wie alle Lust so eitel hier auf Erden!

THE END.

Printed by R. & R. CLARK, *Edinburgh.*

www.ingramcontent.com/pod-product-compliance
Lightning Source LLC
Chambersburg PA
CBHW020807230426
43666CB00007B/904